THE TEARS OF GOD

THE TEARS OF GOD

Our Benevolent Creator and Human Suffering

Wilfrid Harrington, O.P.

A Michael Glazier Book
THE LITURGICAL PRESS
Collegeville, Minnesota

A Michael Glazier Book published by The Liturgical Press

Cover by David Manahan, O.S.B.

1   2   3   4   5   6   7   8   9

Library of Congress Cataloging-in-Publication Data

Harrington, Wilfrid J.
    The tears of God / Wilfrid J. Harrington.
      p. cm.
    "A Michael Glazier book."
    ISBN 0-8146-5006-6
    1. Suffering of God. 2. Theodicy. I. Title.
BT153.S8H37 1992   91-44463
231'.4—dc20   CIP

For
JOAN and MICHAEL

". . . tagann an ghrian i ndiaidh na fearthainne."

CONTENTS

PREFACE

Can one be comfortable with God? Only if one's God is a comfortable God! And, in that case, one has ground for concern. God should be our comfort. But a *comfortable* God is a false God. For most of us there may be little threat in this direction. Our traditional God is an aloof figure—often, a forbidding figure. He has been shunted so far into the realm of perfection that he is made to seem unreal. Strangely, while he is quite firmly presented as one gravely offended by human sin, he has been made to appear unaffected by human suffering.

There is the appalling burden of human suffering. It is a devastating fact that stands as an indictment. How can suffering on such a scale—so much innocent suffering to boot—be compatible with faith in a benevolent Creator? The question is a tormenting one. If one's God is stolidly impassible, never, in any sense, passive or receptive, then there can be no answer short of a blind and desperate act of faith. Yet, there is an answer. The answer is the Cross—but a Cross which makes room for the *real* God and the *real* Jesus.

Biblical metaphor demands that we acknowledge a God who grieves and laments and suffers. The realism of the Christ-event demands that we acknowledge the presence of our God in the suffering and in the death of Jesus. A God who suffers, a God who manifests his divinity on the Cross, can never be a comfortable God. He is a wholly comforting God. He is the God who takes into himself our brokenness. He is the God of compassion who suffers with us—and for us.

This little book is meant to show something of this gracious God. It is no more pretentious in its scope than in its size. The extensive theological footnotes are not for effect; they are designed to undergird the argument of the text. The argument is simple: God is God of compassion. Not a comfortable God—but so eminently comforting.

Wilfrid J. Harrington, O.P.

INTRODUCTION

"**W**e believe in one God, the Father, the Almighty." It may be, indeed it often is, the case that this confident credal statement enshrines a serious misconception of God. To proclaim that one believes in God is not enough. What matters, and matters utterly, is the kind of God in whom one believes. The title "Father" conveys no consistent image of God, while the qualification "almighty" pushes it heavily in one direction, the direction of authority and domination. We speak of God in metaphor. We speak of God anthropomorphically—in human terms. Necessarily so, because we can speak meaningfully of reality only out of our experience. Since, for believers, God is personal, we speak of God in terms of human personality—the only personality we know. Metaphor and imagery are necessary forms of our God-language. All the more reason why we should take our metaphor and imagery seriously.

Metaphor

Biblical metaphor is rich indeed. This is not to say that all metaphors for God are on the same level. Some are of limited significance, for instance, God as rock (Ps 31:2-3)—though it does convey his solid reliability; others are of abiding significance, such as God as parent (Hos 11:1). Certain metaphors for God have priority over others. Some images point to the essential Godness of God—God is love, God is faithful. Other images are time and culturally conditioned—the "wrath" of God, for example. While biblical metaphors are many, the trend has been to settle for a limited fund of metaphors—those judged more "appropriate." The theological tendency has been to draw general conclusions from the

11

metaphors—for instance, God is living, personal. To a large extent, bias in favor of some biblical metaphors rather than others flows from dogmatic presuppositions. The result has been impoverishment—and worse.

It might be argued that the more insidious enemy of God is not atheism but religion! Many atheists reject not God but the travesty-God presented by religion and by the conduct of those who profess to serve God. The true atheist, the one who, calmly and deliberately, rejects the very possibility of a Supreme Being, has to be a person of courage. To struggle through life, without any light at all at the end of the tunnel, is challenging. Better that than a life bolstered by trust in a false God. Such "trust" diminishes one. That is bad enough. What is intolerable is the foisting of a false God on others. In the history of religion, the fostering of false Gods has devastated countless lives. I would make my own the passionate avowal of Edward Schillebeeckx: "I feel very strongly that it is better that there should be no belief in eternal life than that a God should be presented who diminishes people in the here and now, keeps them down and humiliates them politically with an eye to a better hereafter."[1]

False God

The fact remains that false images of God abound—not least among believers. I have become increasingly conscious of the fact. More and more, too, I have come to appreciate the Christian truth that Jesus is the revelation of God. Acceptance of this truth makes two demands: to let Jesus be Jesus and to let God be God. Simple demands, it seems, yet consistently ignored. As a result both Jesus and God get gravely distorted.

Here it will suffice to glance at the travesty "God of the Old Testament." He is held to be a fearsome, distant figure. His devotees trembled before him. The real God of the Bible is someone quite other. Perhaps, deep down, our reluctance to acknowledge this God has something of that discomfiture of man and woman in the garden (Gen 3:8-10): we are reluctant to come face to face with this God. Or, it may be that we fear what may be asked of us. To encounter God: it is a chastening thought. But need we be afraid?

We can, without much difficulty, find some support for this fearsome "God of the Old Testament." In the Bible we encounter human beings and human affairs. Inevitably, we meet with some primitive and mistaken religious notions, some inadequate images of God. When a sometimes unpalatable God is seen in broader setting, he appears in a truer light. The God of Hosea is a God who agonizes over his unfaithful spouse, who will not give her up. God is the Mother who bends to nurse her infant child. Jeremiah can boldly tell his God that his demands are unreasonable. Job can accuse God of indifference to innocent suffering. In short, this travesty figure, the "God of the Old Testament," is sustainable only on the basis of ignorance of, or gross misunderstanding of, the Old Testament.

God, Our Mother

Nowadays it is not uncommon to have God referred to as "Mother." One's first reaction to hearing (or reading) the title may be surprise—perhaps disbelief. Some find the title offensive. The question is: should it be thought inappropriate? In point of fact, it makes quite as much sense to refer to God as Mother as it does to call God Father. God is neither male nor female; God stands apart from such categories. Furthermore, "father" and "mother" describe a *human* reality; and God is not Father or Mother in the same way that humans are such. To call God "Father" is to acknowledge that he is source of our being, of our life, in a manner that is, in some way, comparable to one's parents role in our shaping. In that sense God is Parent. It is due to linguistic convention that God is called "Father" and referred to in male terms. The very recent fashion of naming God "Mother" and of referring to God as "She" is unconventional, but it is theologically respectable. Because of linguistic convention it is not, at present, feasible to discuss God at length in consistently inclusive terms. We must wait for our languages to evolve in that direction.

Indeed, the "motherhood" of God is not a new discovery. It is present, sparingly it is true, but firmly, in the Old Testament.

So, for instance, the unfaithful people of Israel are reminded of who their God is:

> You were unmindful of the Rock that begot you and you forgot the God who gave you birth (Deut 32:18).

"Rock" is a thoroughly macho image; then, startlingly, there is the counter image of the Mother-God, "the God who gave you birth." Again, in a hymn to Yahweh the Redeemer, we have the picture of a long-suffering God being stirred to action: "I will cry out like a woman in travail, I will gasp and pant" (Isa 42:14)—a powerfully female image. Or, Isaiah 66:13: "As one whom his mother comforts, so I will comfort you"—mother-image and mother-love.

These are not the only pertinent texts. Because the Bible comes from and reflects a patriarchal culture, it tends to be male-centred—androcentric. The predominant biblical metaphors for God are taken from male experience, with God being depicted as father, warrior, king, and so on. At the same time, there is an intriguing openness to the use of female images with God, as we have seen, being imaged as birth-giving woman and loving mother. The range of images helps us to become more aware of the goodness of God's ways with us.

Our God is gracious and one does not, by any means, deny graciousness to fatherhood. Still, there is the pervasive conviction that God *is* male. And there is the widely held corollary that maleness reflects God in a way that femaleness cannot. If this were theory only, it might be simply ridiculous. In practice, the attitude has sustained the dominance of men and the subordination of women, not only in society at large but, tragically, in the churches, too. Practical acceptance of the Motherhood of God would go a long way towards assuring that women are *seen* to be what in reality they *are*: just as fully children of God as are their brothers.

The Pathos of God

While female images of the deity—with the implications of that imagery—are not the major concern of this book, they do merit our attention and lead, naturally enough, to another form of neglected imagery—anthropopathic metaphor. Anthropo*pathism* refers to the *pathos* of God: metaphors which refer to the *suffering* of God. And this brings us to my purpose. Such images have been ignored, with the result that an essential aspect of the kind of God that Israel worshipped has been missed. This means neglect of an essential aspect of the God revealed in Jesus.[2]

If we are to be true to the *whole* biblical picture, we shall need to pay far more attention than we had to the metaphors of *pathos*. Neglect of them has contributed, in its measure, to the dominant image of God as a dominating Being. Neglect of them has caused many to turn away, in disgust, from a God who seems to display disdainful unconcern for human suffering. Attention to them would surely have fostered a more caring Church and might have tempered ecclesiastical arrogance. Perhaps. Most importantly, those metaphors of pathos are essential ingredients of a balanced portrait of God. They add, immeasurably, to his attractiveness and counter, effectively, the many false gods of our religious heritage.

There is, surely, something compelling about a God who grieves over a humankind gone astray. A God who suffers because of his people's rejection of him, who suffers with his suffering people, who suffers on behalf of the people, is, indeed, a challenging God. He is, surely, the foolish God discerned by Paul. He is the God who has shown that he is a God not aloof from pain and sorrow and death. He *is* the God of humankind. He is the *kind* of God we need. He is *our* God.

Who, then, is God? Our God is the Father of our Lord Jesus Christ, who has shown himself in the life and cross of Jesus. He is truly the God of the Old Testament, whom Jesus knew and addressed as *Abba*—Father. The difference is that, through the revelation of the Son, *we* see him more clearly. The New Testament brings more sharply and emphatically before us a concerned and caring Parent: "God so loved the world that he gave his only Son" (John 3:16). Our God is the Father who has given us his Son—given us himself. We measure love by our experience of love. We have to measure even divine love by our human standard. To do so, we need to think the unthinkable, believe the unbelievable. God has revealed himself to us in the human person, in the life, death, and resurrection of Jesus of Nazareth. In him God has come to walk with us. In him God has suffered among us and at our hands. He is always the same God, the one God, who speaks to us from the first page of the Bible to the last.

Notes

1. *Church*. The Human Story of God (London: SCM, 1990, 130).

2. Abraham Heschel described the prophets' proclamation of God as *pathetic theology*. The prophets understood themselves and the people in the *pathos* of God. Heschel's view has been put by Jürgen Moltmann: "In his *pathos* the Almighty goes out of himself, entering into the people whom he has chosen. He makes himself a partner in a covenant with his people. In this *pathos,* this feeling for the people which bears his name and upholds his honour in the world, the Almighty is himself ultimately affected by Israel's experience, its acts, its sins and its sufferings. In the fellowship of his covenant with Israel, God becomes capable of suffering. His existence and the history of the people are linked together through the divine pathos. Creation, liberation, covenant, history and redemption spring from the pathos of God. This therefore has nothing to do with the passions of the moody, envious or heroic gods belonging to the mythical world of the sagas. These gods are subject to destiny because of their passions. But the divine passion about which the Old Testament tells us is God's freedom. It is the free relationship of passionate participation. The eternal God takes men and women seriously to the point of suffering with them in their struggles and in being wounded in his love because of their sins" *The Trinity and the Kingdom of God*. The Doctrine of God (London: SCM, 1981) 25–26. See Abraham J. Heschel, *The Prophets* (New York: Harper & Row, 1962).

1
THE GRIEVING GOD
THE GOD OF BEGINNINGS

And the Lord was sorry that he had made humankind on the earth, and it grieved him to his heart (Gen 6:6).

"Let us make MAN in our image, after our likeness" (Gen 1:26). This is the high moment of the primeval story of Genesis 1-11. The earth had been shaped, and the heaven with its lights; the waters had been gathered into their place. Grasses and cereal plants and fruit trees flourished. Birds and fishes teemed; cattle, wild beasts and creeping things roamed the earth. The world was riotously alive. All was good. God looked, complacently, on the works of his word. The world pulsed with life. Yet, there was an emptiness, a silence. There was wanting the crowning glory, the masterpiece. There remained the desire of God, his need of a counterpart. "Let us make human beings in our image." God will not remain alone. He set to creating a creature that would correspond, one with whom he can speak and who would listen. In God's creation human beings are unique in that they are God's counterpart; their *raison d'etre* is their relationship to God.[1] With humans alone, in all creation, can God have dialogue. Because he is a loving God, that dialogue will be free. His counterpart will respond to him in freedom—or not at all. MAN[2] is God's image: his representative, who will administer the earth in his name.

Responsibility

"Have dominion": the commission reflects the relationship of God to creation. MAN is ever God's representative, with a dominion

17

that carries heavy responsibility. The earth has been entrusted to humankind, but it remains God's property: "The earth is the Lord's and all it contains" (Ps 24:1). MAN has been granted no license to exploit—in a destructive sense—nature, to despoil the earth. MAN's special obligation, as image of God, is a call to respect for the natural world. God has concern for *all* of his creation, not only for humankind. Human dominion over the earth is meant to be a wise and benevolent rule so that it may be, in its measure, the sign of God's lordship over his creation. If MAN is unfaithful in his stewardship—which, because he is humanly gifted, will be creative—he not only fails the Creator but betrays the earth he had been created to administer. MAN has authority, but true authority calls for profound respect for the object of authority. And, with the best will in the world, there remains the unknown, the riddle of the whole.[3]

Partners

Earlier than the Priestly writer, the Yahwist had told the story in his own inimitable way.[4] When Yahweh had breathed life into the shape he had moulded of dust from the ground, that human thing became a living being. Formed of dust from the ground, MAN (*adam*) will return to the ground (*adamah*): he is set, inexorably, on a course from birth to death. God made a home for man and gave him a commission to work: a trait of humanness. Man is incomplete. Animals are not adequate for his fulfilment. "I shall make him a helper fit for him" (2:18). "This at last is bone of my bones and flesh of my flesh" (2:23): man has a companion, a partner sharing life to the full. Now there is community—and now there is humanity. "It is not good for man to be alone." Human existence cannot be understood *only* in relationship to God. Human community is God's purpose for humankind. The community of man and woman is the basic shape of community.

"To Be Like God . . ."

Humankind receives a command: "You may freely eat of every tree of the garden; but of the tree of the knowledge of good and evil

you shall not eat" (2:16-17). Law is impersonal; a command sets
up a relationship. MAN is challenged to relate to God in freedom;
it is God's acknowledgment of human freedom. MAN, of his nature, can obey—or disobey. The temptation story (Gen 3) brings
the matter to a head. A talking snake focuses attention on the command: "You shall be like God, knowing good and evil." The
knowledge in question is knowledge of what is useful or harmful
to humankind. Of itself, such knowledge can be beneficial. The
snag is the temptation to "be like God," to overstep the limits
of humanness. God may be lost sight of in the drive after knowledge and the right relationship with God be ruptured. So it is here,
and God is at once on the scene: "Where are you?" MAN is called
to responsibility for his conduct because God intends humans to
be responsible. MAN had sinned and is expelled from the garden.
Now he experiences God as one at a distance, and he has learned
that he is cut off from the possibility of being a god. This is a lesson humankind will have to learn over and over again. Guilty
humankind had endeavored to cover the nakedness of shame. God
takes a hand. Before expelling man and woman from the garden,
he clothed them. MAN need not be ashamed before humankind
nor ashamed before God; he need not constantly feel that he is
sinner. God sends man and woman out into the world free of guilt
feeling.

What has, traditionally, come to be known as "The Fall" is,
really, nothing of the sort. The idea that Genesis 2-3 has to do
with an "original state," a state of ideal innocence, which was for-
feited by sin—thereby involving a "fall" into our present state—
rests on a misunderstanding of the text.[5] The story is concerned
with human existence; it is not dealing with an historical situation.
It faces the question "Why is MAN, created by God, one limited
by death, suffering, toil and sin?" and answers it in its manner.
It does not trace human limitation back to guilt. It does accept
that humankind is alienated from God but not cut off from God.
MAN remains God's creature and enjoys God's care. MAN will
vainly strive to be like God. God's patience will win out: he will
have the last word.

Society

MAN is not only man and woman; there is the community of brothers and sisters. The "man" instanced in Genesis 4 is "man" who stands in a community relationship quite different from that of husband and wife. The community of existence as brothers is not only basic to human living, but it has its negative as well as its positive aspects. "Society is there only when people are together in community. Genesis 4:2-16 shows the two basic social elements: the positive—the division of labor, the negative—the conflicts that spring from rivalry and can lead even to extermination."[6] The tensions show not only in the sibling rivalry illustrated in the Cain and Abel story but follow on the communal arrogance pictured in the Babel narrative.

The Grief of God

In the flood story what is at issue is an awareness that the human race is open to threat: a feeling reinforced by natural disasters like earthquake and flood. We encounter the common view of the ancient world that all reality is ultimately traced to the gods. Even the Hebrew God was thought capable of destructive action. But here is the difference: the grief of Yahweh. "Yahweh was sorry that he had made man on the earth, and it grieved him to his heart. . . . I will blot out man whom I have created from the face of the ground . . . for I am sorry that I have made them" (6:6-7). Sorrow and grief are not acknowledgment of a bad mistake in ever creating humankind; they flow from Yahweh's observation that "the wickedness of man was great in the earth, and every imagination of the thoughts of his heart was only evil continually" (6:5). What is in question is wholesale corruption—to such a degree as to threaten human existence. God *has* to do something about the situation. Yes—but there is the "inconsistency." The first decision, "I will blot out man" is followed by the statement that "Noah found favor in the eyes of the Lord." The conclusion of the Yahwistic story (8:20-22) is Yahweh's abrogation of his decision to destroy. "I will never again curse the ground because of man (a reference to 3:17—'cursed is the ground because of you') neither will I ever again destroy every living creature as I have done" (8:21). Not that he is under any illusion: "for the imagination of man's heart is evil from his youth" (8:21). God has decided to put up with humankind's tendency to evil. One is reminded of Matthew 5:45: "For the Father makes the sun rise on the evil and the good, and sends rain on the just and the unjust."

Mystery of Evil

"The imagination of man's heart is evil from his youth": evil is within humanness, not outside of it. For evil is not only the absence of good; it is, more precisely, the absence of everything human. The origin of evil remains an unsolved mystery—there is no etiology of evil.[7] But it is something within humanness. Satan is a powerful symbol, representing the whole gamut of evil and its infectious presence in the human race. The Christian hope is the restoration of all things in Christ—meaning not only that humanness will be purged of evil but meaning the absolute end of evil itself. The "lake of fire" of Revelation consumes even "the Dragon" (Rev 20:10, 14).

God's Promise

If the Yahwistic flood story ends with sacrifice (Gen 8:20-22) the Priestly story closes with covenant (9:8-17). The "covenant" is God's self-commitment: ". . . never again shall there be a flood to destroy the earth" (9:12). God will go so far as to tie a string about his finger! He not only makes a promise but gives the assurance that he has included a built-in reminder: "I set my bow in the cloud, and it shall be a sign of the covenant between me and the earth." A gracious touch.

We have discovered two coherent flood stories only by unravelling our Genesis text. That text is a third story, woven of the two, a new story with a drift and a point beyond either. It is fascinating to see how the final editor has proceeded. He has made little or no attempt to iron out discrepancies. Instead, he has given the ancient story a fresh shape. And he has given it a very firm centre: "God remembered Noah" (8:1). That verse is a watershed. Just look at the sequence: violence (6:9-10), resolve to destroy (6:13-22), command to enter the ark (7:1-10), the flood (7:11-24); *God's remembrance of Noah* (8:1); receding flood (8:1-14), command to leave the ark (8:15-19), resolve to preserve order (8:20-22), covenant blessing and peace (9:1-17). Up to 8:1 there is a movement towards chaos, while a remnant is saved. After 8:1 there is movement towards a new creation with Noah and his family as seed of a new humankind. It is a powerful new story, a more firm message of promise and hope.[8]

"Let us make a name for ourselves . . ."

Humankind gets into its stride and goes its wayward way. "Let us build ourselves a city and a tower with its top in the heavens and let us make a name for ourselves" (11:4). A story of human ambition, a story of the perennial temptation to be like God, to reach to the heavens through human achievement. Vain endeavor. This is not to say that human ambition within measure and authentic human achievement are reprehensible. The inescapable truth is that humans are creatures and can find fulfilment only within creaturely limits. That truth is seen in the call of Abraham (12:1-3). His call is the beginning of the way of God with humankind in history. It shows the contrast between unbridled human ambition and the way of God. "Let us make a name for ourselves. . . . I will bless you, and make your name great" (11:4; 12:2). Where the arrogant men of Babel had sought to go it alone, Abraham is now granted the "name," that is, the fame, to which they had aspired. Human greatness is with God, never apart from God, because it must be within the realm of creaturehood. "To be like God" is vain, and always disastrous.

God's Risk

"Let us make MAN." God had embarked on a path of folly. God was being true to God. To create a creature who is free, free even to say "No!" to the Creator, shows that he really is God. Irenaeus had observed, perceptively: *Gloria Dei, vivens homo*—God's glory is MAN fully alive. He had wanted humans to be free because he had wanted dialogue. He had desired a counterpart with whom he could converse—who would listen—and talk back. He had sought a free relationship. God is not free to create God. Human freedom must be the freedom of a creature. Limitation is not arbitrary but wholly in the nature of things; it is in service of freedom.[9]

In the ancient creation stories—much older than those in the Bible—where gods are created, where some gods are lesser than others, humans are destined to minister to the gods. The biblical view is radically different:

> Where God is unique . . . then this unique being which is not God, namely the individual and his history in the world, becomes of great importance. The creation of human beings in the image of God, a common creation motif, acquires a special meaning in this context; a human being created in the image of God is the unique expression of the unique God.[10]

This fact gives humankind unique status and unparalleled dignity. Only a God who is *God* could dare to be so magnanimous.

God had taken a risk—and paid the price. He would respect, respect utterly, the freedom of his creature. Sadly, he would come to observe that the thoughts and inclinations of humans are perverse. Sadly, he would regret that he had made humankind on earth. But he would never again destroy. God had come to terms with humankind. It is the story-teller's way of acknowledging the human reality, the fact of human contingency and human freedom.[11] The flood was the "wrath of God" on human sin. Later, it would be understood that there is no "wrath" in God. But even now, this God of Genesis, his "wrath" spent, a sadder and wiser God, has determined that "never again shall there be a flood to destroy the earth." He will bear with humankind however evil their bent. He will have the last word. Because, paradoxically, our God is the *Deus humanissimus,* a thoroughly human God. Because he is God of salvation—and human salvation is all about becoming thoroughly human.

The God who did not will to be alone has created humankind. He would have dialogue. He could not create God, but he would have a counterpart. From that human race, summoned forth in freedom, issued the one who responded, wholly. In him, the perfect response to God, God could be, God would be, God in history. God could, God now would, enter into human joy and human sorrow. God could, God would, weep in concert with human woe. God would have compassion with women and men in their pain and in their death. "God remembered Noah": he would henceforth bear with humankind. "The Lord said to Abram": he launched his plan to save humankind. "He did not spare his own Son": he showed that he really is God *for us*.

Notes

1. "The uniqueness of human beings consists in their being God's counterparts. The relationship to God is not something which is added to human existence; humans are created in such a way that their very existence is intended to be their relationship to God. . . .

"One can discern in Gen 1 a gradual ascent—toward the creation of human beings. It moves toward the decision to create humans and to the phrase that God created them in his image. This is the basis of the history that the Old Testament narrates, the history of God with his people. When what is told about Jesus Christ in the New Testament is understood as the fulfilment of the Old Testament, the reason is that something decisive for humankind has taken place in him. When God created human beings so that something may happen between God and these humans, then what is told about Christ in the New Testament is the decisive middle point of this happening." Claus Westermann, *Genesis 1–11. A Commentary* (Minneapolis/London: Augsburg/SPCK, 1984) 158, 177.

2. In Genesis 1 the Hebrew *ha-adam* is humankind: man and woman. The difficulty lies in finding a way, which is not intolerably ponderous, of conveying this meaning over some pages. I have opted for capitalization: MAN.

3. "And God saw everything that he had made, and behold, it was very good" (Gen 1:31).

"It was God's judgment that creation was good. It can never be our judgment, the fruit of our own experience. Our knowledge and experience are always limited by the unexplained and the incomprehensible. We can speak about creation then only with reference to the creator for whom it presents no riddle" C. Westermann, *op. cit.,* 174–175.

4. The Yahwist is the conventional designation of the tenth-century B.C. author of an important strand of the Pentateuch—the Yahwistic tradition. The name derives from the fact that the author consistently uses the proper name "Yahweh" of God.

The Priestly writers (priests of the Jerusalem Temple) account for much of the Pentateuch material and gave its final form to the Pentateuch (probably fifth-century B.C.). The two strands that make up our Genesis 1–11 display the distinctive styles and concerns of the Yahwistic and Priestly writings.

5. "The basic mistake of many misconceptions about creation lies in the fact that finitude is felt to be a flaw. . . . There is a feeling that coming and going, mortality, failure, mistakes and ignorance should not be part of the normal condition of our humanity, and from the beginning people should be endowed with all kinds of 'supernatural' gifts like omniscience and immortality, which they are then thought to have lost because of the primal fall. On a precise reading, it emerges that the Genesis story sets out to make a protest precisely against such conceptions, albeit in mythical terms. If God is creator, then he creates that which is not-divine, that which is completely other than himself, in other words, finite things. Creatures are not replicas of God. The Jewish and Christian creation faith saw this very clearly, though we have to concede that the conceptions of creation in it have often become very distorted under alien influences, even by many Christians. . . . Humanity and the world are not the result of a fall, an apostasy from God, nor are they a failure, much less a testing ground in expectation of better times. If God is the creator, then the creation is of course not-God; it is other than God." Edward Schillebeeckx, *God Among Us. The Gospel Proclaimed* (New York: Crossroad, 1983) 92–93.

6. C. Westermann, *op. cit.,* 318.

7. "When J [the Yahwist] allows the man and the woman to be led astray by the clever snake, creature of God, he is saying that it is not possible to know the origin of evil. We are at a complete loss in face of the fact that God has created a being that can lead people to disobedience. The origin of evil remains a complete mystery. The most important thing that J has to say here is that there is no etiology for the problem of evil; a mythical explanation which pinpoints the origin would destroy this." C. Westermann, *op. cit.,* 239.

8. Bernhard W. Anderson, "From Analysis to Synthesis: The Interpretation of Genesis 1–11," *Journal of Biblical Literature* 97 (1978) 23–39.

9. "To enjoy and love what is worldly in the world, what is human in man, is to enjoy and love what makes God God. God's glory lies in the happiness and the well-being of mankind in the world: this seems to be the best definition of what creation means. Furthermore, creation is not a chronological event, somewhere at the beginning, but a lasting, dynamic event. For us that means that God wills to be the origin, here and now, of the worldliness of the world and the humanity of mankind—that he wants to be with us in and with our finite involvement in this world." E. Schillebeeckx, *op. cit.,* 94.

10. C. Westermann, *op. cit.,* 67.

11. "God can never be the absolute origin of man's humanity, in other words he cannot be a creator, if he makes man only the one who implements a blueprint predetermined by the divine architect." (E. Schillebeeckx, *op. cit.,* 95).

2
THE SUFFERING GOD
THE GOD OF LAMENTS

Israel, though people of Yahweh, had absorbed much of the "common theology" of the Ancient Near East—a theology of strict retribution. That theology envisaged an ordered world and upheld that order. The god rewarded those with whom he was pleased and punished those who displeased him. Readily, this sustaining of cosmic order was deployed to legitimate political order. Legitimation of structure, defence of the status quo, became a major function of theology. A convenient match was established between the divine order and the human government structure—markedly so in the Judaean theology of David and the Temple. Jerusalem was David's city; the presence of the Temple made it the Zion of Yahweh. The Davidic king was "son of God"; the Davidic monarchy reflected the regime of Yahweh. Indeed, the kings of Israel (while the northern kingdom lasted) would, too, claim divine support. In such a situation the status quo was hardly open to criticism. If one stepped out of line, the only manner of rehabilitation was by way of repentant submission to the established order. It was simply assumed that the order was right; to challenge the system was tantamount to blasphemy.

Voices of Protest

There came, however, a recognition that political and religious power could be unjust and oppressive. There were voices of protest. Injustice must be recognized where it is and acknowledged for what it is, and faced. In a world-view in which everything was traced back to God, this meant challenging God himself. There was challenge, not only of the structure, but of the God who allegedly upheld the structure. And there was the suspicion that God did not necessarily stand over the system. It was a recognition that Israel's God was not a God who would brook no challenge but one who might be directly challenged. A God, indeed, who invited challenge. There was need for sharp critique, need for complaint to God—even *about* God. Israel refused to settle for the way things are. God looked for obedience—responsible, free, obedience. God wanted to be challenged. This was a decisive turning point which found expression in Israel's practice of lament.[1]

Moses

Moses was leader and mediator. He was very conscious of his role of intercessor, his service to his people. In that task he was outspoken and generous. He had been sent to free the people. Yet, his approach to Pharaoh seemed only to aggravate their plight. He complained, exasperatedly: "You have not delivered your people at all!" (Exod 5:23). The same Moses is prepared to put his neck on the block. If Yahweh will not forgive the people's infidelity, then: "blot me, I pray you, out of your book which you have written" (32:32). Moses reminds his God that the perverse crowd left in his charge is *God's* people—*he* might try looking after them for a change! (33:12-13). When Yahweh called his bluff, Moses promptly pulled in his horns. God proposed to destroy the rebellious people and make Moses father of a new people, but Moses will have none of it (Num 14:13-19). Like a later Jeremiah, while he huffed and puffed, Moses got on with the job.

Jeremiah

Jeremiah had never wanted to be a prophet (1:16; 17:16; 20:7-9), and he continued to discuss the trials of his office with Yahweh throughout his life. He was overwhelmed with the sheer burden, the humanly impossible demands of his task. Nor was he, at all, satisfied to accept, uncritically, traditional theological positions. He struggled, as the author of Job was to struggle, with the problem of retribution (12:1) and he asserted the principle of individual (as against collective) responsibility (31:29-30). But, mostly, it was his own prophetic office that was his burden, and it was indeed a yoke far heavier and more painful than that of any other prophet. He needed, all the more, the support of his God. His obedience was so much the greater because of his questioning, because he felt its chafing, because it led to a feeling of being abandoned.

There is another dimension to the suffering of a Jeremiah: a prophet's life reflects the divine life. If to hear the word of a prophet is to hear God, to see a suffering prophet is to look upon a suffering God. For a prophet not only speaks the word of God, he embodies it. And the prophet suffers precisely as servant of God:

> God is present and active not only in and through what the prophet speaks, but also in what he does and, indeed, in who he is. The prophet's life is an embodiment of the Word of God; the prophet is a vehicle for divine immanence. The prophet's life is thus theomorphic. By so participating in the story of God, his life is shaped into the image and likeness of God. The people thus not only hear the Word of God from the prophet, they *see* the Word of God enfleshed in their midst. In and through the suffering of the prophet, the people both hear and see God immersed in human experience. Through the prophet, Israel relates not only to a God who speaks, but also to a God who appears.[2]

When Jeremiah declares. "I have become a laughing-stock all the day; every one mocks me," he acknowledges not only his own rejection, but the people's rejection of God himself. Over the cry of the prophet we can hear the anguish of God in face of the broken relationship with his people. In the pain of the prophet we can discern a God who suffers on behalf of the people.[3] We see a God who yearns for their return, a God who wants to restore the broken marrriage. This is most prominent in Hosea.

Hosea

Hosea was a man who had known the pain of love—*chagrin d'amour*. He had loved and married a woman who had proved unfaithful. His love was steadfast and he won her back (1-3). He learned that faithfulness in face of unfaithfulness is costly indeed. His own painful journey through love gave him a startling glimpse into the heart of his loving God. So close is the link between experience and revelation, that it is chapter 2—the love affair of Yahweh and Israel—which leads to a keener grasp of the prophet's personal tragedy.

In sorrow Yahweh had divorced his spouse: "she is not my wife and I am not her husband" (2:2). Here, as at Babel where his will to scatter humankind out of his sight (Gen 11:1-9) faltered in his call of Abraham to a new beginning (12:1-3), and at the flood when his grim decision to "blot out man whom I created from the face of the ground for I am sorry that I have made them" flows directly into the declaration, "but Noah found favor in the eyes of the Lord" (6:7-8), God is inconsistent. Ever, God's weak side is his love. Divorced Israel may be—price of unfaithfulness. In God's eyes she is still his spouse, and he will not give her up:

> Therefore, behold, I will allure her, and bring her into the wilderness and speak tenderly to her. . . . And she shall answer as in the days of her youth, as at the time when she came out of the land of Egypt. . . . And I will betroth you to me forever; I will betroth you to me in righteousness and in justice, in steadfast love and in mercy. I will betroth you to me in faithfulness and you shall know the Lord.
>
> Hos 2:14-15, 19-20

Hosea harked back to the wilderness and the entry into the land. He looked to the graciousness of Yahweh and noted the rank ingratitude of Israel (9:10; 11:1-12; 13:4-6). Some might see in his own tragedy the image of the long-suffering spouse. Some who, like the prophet, had known the joy and pain of love.

The Hosea who did not hesitate to present God as Spouse of his people could also daringly picture God as Mother of a first-born child:

> When Israel was a child, I loved him, and out of Egypt I called my son . . . It was I who taught Ephraim to walk; I was to them like one who lifts a child to the breasts . . . and I bent down to nurse them.
>
> Hos 11:3-4

This love, too, meets ingratitude. The poem had begun on a sad note: "The more I called them the more they went from me" (11:2). They deserve to be sent back to Egypt again. God would leave them where God had found them. And she would—but for her vulnerable love:

> How can I give you up, O Ephraim? . . . My heart recoils within me, my compassion grows warm and tender . . . I will not again destroy Ephraim. For I am God and not man, and I will not come to destroy.
>
> Hos 11:8-9

"I am God and not man"—"man" is not *adam* ("humanity") but *ish*: specifically male. Yahweh is rejecting *male* behavior. She is not going to act with stern anger and destroy her people; strong maternal emotions resist such conduct on her part.[4] In chapter 11, then, Yahweh as mother is a warm image of God for Hosea. The mother-love of God shines through the father-love of a prophet.[5]

Job

Job is an outstanding example of challenge. His harrowing journey was from faith to faith. It was an epic journey, though he had not stirred from his seat on the ash-heap. He groped through a dark night, throwing down the gauntlet to that elusive God along the way. His quest for an answer to the perennial problem of innocent suffering is as pressing in our day as ever it was in his. Our perception, not shared by the author of Job, of an afterlife and of retribution beyond death, should not dispose us to seek a facile answer to the problem. The extraordinarily harsh protest of Job 9:19-24 decisively nullifies the dominant theology. For, Job has definitively concluded that the theology of strict retribution does not work:

> If it is a contest of strength, behold him!
> If it is a matter of justice, who can summon him?
> Though I am innocent, my own mouth would condemn me;
> though I am blameless, he would prove me perverse . . .
> it is all one; therefore, I say,
> he destroys both the blameless and the wicked.

> When disaster brings sudden death,
> he mocks at the calamity of the innocent.

There is an even more outrageous passage—24:1-12. Job asks in exasperation: "Why are not times of judgment kept by the Almighty?" Then he describes the arrogant oppression of the oppressor and the helpless suffering of the oppressed. At the end he hurls his challenge at God:

> From out of the city the dying groan,
> and the soul of the wounded cries for help;
> yet God pays no attention to their prayer!

The sheer honesty is heart-rending. How utterly different from another view:

> I was young and now I am old,
> but I have never seen the just man forsaken
> nor his children begging for bread.
>
> Ps 37:25

This is pathetic: a desperate clinging to a doctrinaire position in face of the evidence. But if your theology is neatly systematic—and your God predictible—you will, perforce, sacrifice fact to theory.

For Job the doctrine of retribution did not work. And, contrary to his traditional theology, he learned that there could be suffering which did not flow from sin. More agonizing than his attempt to cope with these problems was the absence of God. Job keeps crying out to a God who will not answer—even summoning that God to court. His experience is a classic instance of the "dark night of the soul" described by later mystics. God had not withdrawn, but Job *felt* that he had. In reality he was, in his search, growing closer all the time to that hidden God. His situation shouted that God was uncaring—callous even. Job's sturdy faith will not accept that to be so.

In his frustration and anger Job came to glimpse the God veiled from the eyes of his theologically complacent friends. In wonder he recognized that God can be wholly preoccupied with one suffering human. He learned that the seemingly aloof and silent God was a God who willed to be within the human world:

God desires closeness; intimacy is God's goal. Further, God is one who chooses to be so present in the finitude and frailty of a human being—indeed, a powerless human being as power is usually conceived. He is one who startles the nations, for who would have believed that the arm of the Lord was revealed in such a one as this (Isa 53:1)? In and through such individuals, God thereby identifies with frail people. And it is thereby shown that God is not a suffering-at-a-distance God; God enters into the suffering of all creatures and experiences their life. Moreover, this experience means entering into a death-filled situation with the people, not only so that God can experience it, but so that God can work creatively from within it and raise them up to be a part of a new world (cf. Ezek 37).[6]

God Laments

The laments to God, and complaints about God to God, not only witness to a strikingly personal understanding of, and attitude toward, God, but prepare for laments *of* God. God catches up the human cry and makes it his own—a smooth transition from personal cries of the prophets. God had chosen Israel as his own and had made a covenant with his people. Now, he suffers when he is spurned and rejected by his people. He suffers because he is, and will be, faithful. He recalls his promise to Noah and rephrases it, in stronger terms, in favor of Israel:

> As I swore that the waters of Noah
> should no more go over the earth,
> so I have sworn that I will not be angry with you . . .
> my steadfast love shall not depart from you . . . .
>
> Isa 54:9-10

His grieving is not only, nor mainly, a response to unfaithfulness; it will be a way of salvation for his people.

God will poignantly conjure up what might have been. The Book of Isaiah, for instance, opens on a note of bewilderment:

> Children have I reared and brought up,
> but they have rebelled against me.
> The ox knows its owner,
> and the ass its master's crib;

> but Israel does not know,
> my people does not understand.
>
> Isa 1:2-3

He is a father, cut to the heart by the ingratitude of children. He knows anguish:

> My people have forgotten me
> days without number.
>
> Jer 2:32

He suffers the pang of unrequited love:

> I thought you would call me, My Father,
> and would not turn from following me.
> Surely, as a faithless wife leaves her husband,
> so have you been faithless to me, O house of Israel.
>
> Jer 3:20

Here the easy juxtaposition of parent-child and husband-wife metaphors alerts us to the common theme of love and assures us that a loving God experiences the pain as well as the rapture of love. God calls out, repeatedly—but in vain:

> I was ready to be sought by those who did not ask for me;
> I was ready to be found by those who did not seek me.
> I said, "Here am I, here am I,"
> to a nation that did not call on my name.
> I spread out my hands all day
> to a rebellious people.
>
> Isa 65:1-2

Most poignant of all is Hosea 11 which unveils, as we have noted, the mother side of God:

> It was I who taught Ephraim to walk,
> I took them up in my arms;
> but they did not know that I . . .
> lifted them up like a little child to the breast,
> and bent down to nurse them.
>
> Hos 11:3-4

Here is mother pathos at the heart of God: she loves her child and will not, because she cannot, let go.[7] God's suffering is not for herself; it is for the erring and suffering child—a rebellious people.

Steadfast Love

In all of this—and one offers but a hint of God's laments—God is never one who stands calmly aloof, impervious to being spurned and rejected by his people. He is one who grieves over a broken relationship—grieves for the tragic unfaithful partner. "In spite of the suffering God undergoes, God's salvific will does not waver; God's steadfast love endures forever. In this respect God offers the supreme example of what to do with suffering."[8] God treats the human party in the relationship with total seriousness and scrupulously respects human freedom. His patience is inexhaustible; he cannot be worn down. He is determined to restore the relationship. He may withdraw, but he will not finally give up. The breach will be healed.

God Suffers

God suffers *because* of his people's rejection of him; he is deeply wounded by the broken relationship. His steadfast will endures as he bears with the human party. He is not legalistic, never vindictive; he seeks salvation, not judgment, life, not death. His extraordinary patience takes him to unexpected lengths in his striving to heal the breached relationship. God suffers *with* the suffering people. He becomes a mourner—a God in sackcloth and ashes. For God to mourn with the mourning means not only divine compassion; it means that mourning must one day cease. God mourns because Israel has died, but death is the way to rebirth. God mourns over non-Israelite peoples, weeps for the sufferers of the world. The tears of God are seed of new life. God suffers *for* the people. Because God is not a legalist, he chooses to bear the people's sins. He is *wearied* by the burden of their sin. By assuming that burden he gives them room to breathe and raises them from death.[9] The suffering of God is the birthpangs of new creation, the birthing of a new order. God is pregnant with that new order. This time

God brings forth not a new people of God but the whole of humankind.

There is ever the human temptation to construct a God in our image. There is the temptation of the establishment to foster a God who sustains the status quo. These laments of God are God's own protest. He will suffer manipulation—but he will not suffer in silence. He is God of men and women; the cause of humanity is the cause of God himself.[10] To that end, God is prepared to be the rejected and outcast one.

Notes

1. "The moment when Israel found the nerve and the faith to risk an assault on the throne of God with complaint was a decisive moment against legitimation. The lament is a dramatic, rhetorical, liturgical act of speech which makes clear that Israel will no longer be a submissive, subservient recipient of decrees from the throne. There is a bold movement and voice from Israel's side which does not blindly and docilely accept, but means to have its dangerous say, even in the face of God." Walter Brueggemann, "A Shape for Old Testament Theology, I. Structure Legitimation; II. Embrace of Pain," *The Catholic Biblical Quarterly* 47 (1985) 28–46; 395–415; here p. 400 is cited.

2. Terence E. Fretheim, *The Suffering of God* (Philadelphia: Fortress, 1984) 165.

3. To speak of God as one who suffers is to speak in metaphor, or analogically. God does not suffer in the same way that humans do. There is always in the metaphor a large element that is discontinuous with the reality which is God. But, if one is to take seriously biblical language and imagery, one must acknowledge a God who suffers and mourns. Later Greek notions of divine impassibility, ideas alien to biblical thought, must not be allowed to obscure that comforting truth.

4. See Helen Schüngel-Straumann, "Gott als Mutter in Hosea 11," *Theologische Quartalschrift* 166:2 (1986) 119–34.

5. "The striking note of Hosea is that, whereas the common human reaction in such a situation would be to give up, God's love is such that she cannot let go. The parental pathos in the heart of God! The complaint against the children has been spoken; the word of complete abandonment is expected. But then, in Hos 11:8 in particular, there is that pouring out of mingled sorrow and love which prevents the final ruin of the children. Thus, God's Godness is revealed in the way in which, amid all the sorrow and anger, God's salvific purposes remain unclouded and the steadfastness of divine love endures forever." T. E. Fretheim, *op. cit.,* 120.

6. T. E. Fretheim, *op. cit.*, 166. The observation of Jürgen Moltmann is pertinent: "It is in suffering that the whole human question about God arises; for incomprehensible suffering calls the God of men and women in question. The suffering of a single innocent child is an irrefutable rebuttal of the notion of the almighty and kindly God in heaven. For a God who lets the innocent suffer and who permits senseless death is not worthy to be called God at all. Wherever the suffering of the living in all its manifold forms pierces our consciousness with its pain, we lose our childish primal confidence and our trust in God. The person who is torn by suffering stands alone. There is no explanation of suffering which is capable of obliterating his pain, and no consolation of a higher wisdom which could assuage it. The person who cries out in pain over suffering has a dignity of his own which neither men nor gods can rob him of. The story of Job makes this evident; and since that time no theology can fall below Job's level. The theology of 'Job's friends' is confuted. Does Job have any real theological friend except the crucified Jesus on Golgotha?" *The Trinity and the Kingdom of God.* The Doctrine of God (London: SCM, 1981) 47–48.

7. "God is not simply father; God is a certain kind of father. God is a loving father, always (Hos 11:1). And God is not simply mother; God is a certain kind of mother. God is a mother who will not forget her children, ever (Isa 49:15)." T. E. Fretheim, *op. cit.*, 12.

8. T. E. Fretheim, *op. cit.*, 124.

9. "It is clear that human sin has not been without cost for God, and that cost is due in significant part to the fact that God has chosen to bear the people's sins rather than deal with them on strictly legal terms. For God to assume such a burden, for God to continue to bear the brunt of Israel's rejection, meant continued life for the people." T. E. Fretheim, *op. cit.*, 148.

10. "God's glory is human happiness. But this happiness is not simply an individual concern. . . . This means that the believer's concern for God's honour is also a struggle for more justice in the world, a commitment to a new earth and an environment in which human beings can live fuller lives. If Christian salvation is salvation of and for human beings—men and women with flesh and blood, who by their very nature are directed towards creating free society for free human beings, this means that Christian salvation is not simply the salvation of souls but the healing, making whole, wholeness, of the whole person, the individual and society, in a natural world which is not abused. Thus Christian salvation also comprises ecological, social and political aspects, though it is not exhausted by these. Christian salvation is more than that, but it is that too." Edward Schillebeeckx, *God Among Us.* The Gospel Proclaimed (New York: Crossroad, 1983) 100.

"The most serious heresy of European Christianity, especially in the last few centuries, has been the reduction of the gospel to little more than the salvation of souls. I make bold to call it a heresy. Technically I suppose I would have to say that it was a material heresy rather than a formal heresy because it was not deliberate. European Christians, as far as one knows, did not choose to go into heresy, they simply drifted into it. Perhaps some of them could be accused of culpable ignorance. I don't know and at this stage it doesn't really matter." Albert Nolan, *God In South Africa*. The Challenge of the Gospel (Grand Rapids/London: Eerdmans/CIIR, 1988) 108–9.

3
THE CRUCIFIED GOD
THE GOD OF JESUS

"Let us run with perseverance the race that is set before us, looking to Jesus the pioneer and perfecter of our faith" (Heb 12:1-2). For the author of Hebrews, faith in Jesus, the High Priest "seated at the right hand of the throne of God" (12:2) is what gives meaning to the Christian way. At the same time, no other New Testament writer, perhaps, has stressed more than he the humanity of this heavenly high priest. For, he has in sight a specific historical person: Jesus of Nazareth. Christianity is not founded on myth. Yet, what came to be, after New Testament times, was ahistorical Christology displaying little of the vulnerable Jesus who died on a cross. Even when the earthly Jesus was kept in view, there has been a tendency to detach the death of Jesus from his life and to detach the resurrection of Jesus from his career and death. To do so is to ignore the challenge of the prophet Jesus and, ultimately, to fail to grasp the saving significance of his death and the true meaning of his resurrection. The life of Jesus of Nazareth is the key to what Christianity is all about.

In the *man* Jesus we meet *God.* That is the astounding truth which stands at the heart of Christianity. It is a truth that Christian theology has wrestled with from the first. The task is formidable, and it should not surprise that some Christological endeavor has not been helpful nor that formulas of the past might not be particularly enlightening in our day. Before going on to look at Jesus as the revelation of God, it is expedient to clear the Christological deck.

The Word Became Flesh

A traditional starting-point of Christology is the Johannine state-ment *ho logos sarx egeneto*—the Word became flesh, became a human person (Jn 1:14). *Logos* (Word) is, within God, the real possibility for the existence of anything or anyone outside him; it is a form of relatedness which a personal God has with a person or persons in our world.[1] The Word is God's eternal commitment to be per-sonally present in history. God wills to share his own life and his very self. This means that, one day, there will be a human being in whom God will take to himself all of the weakness and vulnera-bility of the human condition. Jesus is the concrete shape and form which God's eternal intent has taken. God seeks his own counter-part, the image and likeness of himself—and finds him in Jesus. Jesus of Nazareth—not the Word—is the perfect counterpart and the very "otherness" of God.[2]

As for Jesus, aware of the call of God, conscious of the fatherly love of God, he knows himself to be the one whom God has sought as his counterpart from all eternity. He accepts his role of *Son*. The definitive answer to God's decision not to be alone was spoken, in freedom, by a human person. To Jesus God could say, "My Son" and hear the spontaneous response, "Abba." The mystery of Jesus is that in him God communicates himself in a full and un-restricted way. And the divinity of Jesus means that he is the human person who is the perfect counterpart of God and, therefore, that he is the manifestation and presence of God himself in the world.[3]

The Greek Tradition

In Jesus of Nazareth, God is really and truly present. That is the great Christian truth. But, to seek to define the mysterious nature of Jesus is a precarious endeavor.[4] Not alone have such attempts been made but, for centuries, it has been assumed that the fifth-century Council of Chalcedon had spoken the definitive Christo-logical Word—all that remained was commentary. Christology be-came, in practice, a subtle word-game around the formula of Chalcedon. The question to be answered at Chalcedon was whether God's salvation had been given, once for all, in the man Jesus. Be-cause the answer had to be Yes, and because salvation is of God, it had to be asserted, in the technical language of the day, that God himself was present in the man Jesus. That had been said, long before, by Paul: "God was in Christ, reconciling the world to himself" (2 Cor 5:19). Arguably, this Pauline statement is the very best Christological statement. And it joins soteriology with Christology.

Chalcedon gave its answer. What we, at the close of this twentieth century, need to face is that the philosophical thought-world (Middle Platonic) and Greek terminology of Chalcedon are foreign to us—in a way that the language of Paul is not. Our English terms nature, substance, person (these are the terms used in traditional Christology) do not at all mean what the corresponding Greek terms *physis, ousia, hypostasis* meant for fourth-fifth century Greeks. The argument that the Councils of Nicaea (325) and Chalcedon asserted that Jesus Christ is "of one substance with the Father" or that in him there are "two natures and one person" is invalid—simply because the words "substance," "nature," "person" are English words with meanings quite different from the terms they are supposed to translate. The recent change in the Creed from "one in substance with" to "one in being with," while it is an admission of the semantic problem, is no help. A Schillebeeckx can declare: "As a theologian, I would prefer not to use the term 'one-in-being' any more, because of its special and historically conditioned background."[5] People of our day and culture do not, spontaneously, think of approaching the mystery of Jesus by raising the question of the "nature" or "substance" of Jesus. An approach that was congenial to Christians of the fourth to the sixth centuries of our era is not so for us. We need to use a theological language we can understand.

The situation has been aggravated by the fact that it is not Chalcedon, but a certain interpretation of it, that has dominated mediaeval and later Christology. Thus *anhypostasia,* a denial that Jesus is a human person, goes beyond anything in Chalcedon. Ironically, while the concern of the Council was defense of the true humanness of Jesus (as the one in whom God had given salvation) the effect of the retention of its language of person and nature—only marginally intelligible, if at all, to people of our day—has been to turn Jesus into an alien among us.[6] After this brief essay in Christology, we look at the Jesus of the Gospels.

Jesus of Nazareth

In literary terms "characters" are not the same as people. In day-to-day life we know one another imperfectly. I may guess at your thoughts; I cannot really know what you are thinking. Characters can be transparent. The narrator may fully expose a character to his reader, can permit the reader to get inside the character. Alternatively, he can present a "true" picture of any character. The Gospels, in which Jesus is a literary character—always the main character—make him known to us more profoundly than he, as a person, was in fact known to his contemporaries. This distinction between "character" and "person" is important. Jesus of Nazareth is a thoroughly historical person. He was a first-century Palestinian Jew who carried out what—he was convinced—was a God-given mission to his people. He was rejected and was condemned and executed by an alliance of Jewish religious and Roman political authorities. The "character" Jesus of the Gospels is this Jesus now perceived in the light of resurrection-faith. We encounter the person Jesus filtered through the stories.

Disciple of the Baptist

The starting-point for any account of the ministry of Jesus is his encounter with John the Baptist: the call which Jesus heard when he was baptized by John and to which he responded. On the evidence it may be argued that Jesus had been, for some time, a disciple of the Baptist. But Jesus was to follow his own way. John was a prophet of doom who preached a "baptism of repentance for the forgiveness of sins" (Mark 1:4). Jesus proclaimed: "the kingdom of God is at hand" (1:15). Where John prophesied the judgment of God, Jesus prophesied the salvation of God. Hearing, in prison, of the activity of Jesus, a perplexed John sent two of his disciples to investigate. Jesus' reply was: "Go and tell John what you have seen and heard; the blind receive their sight, the lame walk, lepers are cleansed, and the deaf hear, the poor have the good news preached to them" (Luke 7:22). One can read between the lines. John is being told that there is another prophetic message, another prophetic style. At some point Jesus, disciple of the Baptist, had struck out on his own. The point seems to have been reached with Jesus' reception of *sinners* into the kingdom.

Friend of Sinners

> Now the tax collectors and sinners were all drawing near to hear him. And the Pharisees and the scribes murmured, saying, "This man receives sinners and eats with them" (Luke 15:1-2).

This is Luke's setting for the three parables of mercy: the Lost Sheep, the Lost Coin, the Prodigal Son. He has Jesus being accused of associating with tax collectors—quislings, collaborators with Rome. The more serious charge is associating with sinners. It is important to understand what is meant by "sinners." Not alone was the insult "friend of sinners" thrown in Jesus' face; more seriously, it was one of the charges that eventually led to his death. An initial problem is that the term "sinners" has regularly been taken in too broad a sense—indeed in a quite incorrect way, linked to misconception of Pharisaic attitudes.

In the Gospels the Pharisees, for historical and polemical reasons, get a bad press. They are cast as legalistic rigorists with little respect for people, with contempt for ordinary folk. This is less than fair. Jesus had a good deal in common with Pharisees. And, where the Gospels might seem to give the impression that the Pharisees are those mainly responsible for the death of Jesus, it was, in fact, the Jerusalem priestly authorities (not Pharisees) who, together with Roman authorities, engineered the death of Jesus. The prevalent view of Pharisees has exaggerated their influence and misrepresented their religious outlook. In the eyes of Pharisees, it is maintained, all who did not live according to the standards of meticulous Pharisaic observance of Torah (Law) were "sinners." Furthermore, it is claimed, Pharisees would regard sinners as beyond redemption. The fact is, the Pharisees were a minority group and they had nothing like the influence they are credited with having over the ordinary people. There is no reason to doubt that they and Jesus had serious differences. An embracing difference was in regard to the "tradition of the elders"—a large body of, mainly, ritual observance added to the obligations of Torah. This was, by and large, rejected by Jesus on the principle that "the sabbath is made for man, not man for the sabbath." He, consistently, put people above the demands of religion. Pharisees were keenly aware of God's mercy. They knew that God looked for and welcomed repentance. But they were quite clear that there were conditions surrounding forgiveness.

Given the Pharisees' perception of themselves as people of the law, they would count themselves guardians of the law and of the ancestral customs. Zeal for the law became an identity marker of the "sect" of the Pharisees. It is reasonable, then, to take "sinners" as a *functional term,* describing those whose conduct was regarded as unacceptable to a sectarian mentality. Viewed against this background, passages like Mark 2 and 7 fit quite well into the historical situation of Jesus' ministry.

This brings us back to the conduct of Jesus and to the basis of the serious charge against him. A welcome, on his part, for repentant sinners who had made amends, who had "paid their debt to society," would have been quite acceptable to the "righteous"— whatever else they might have thought of Jesus. The scandal was that he associated with sinners and rejoiced in their company. He did not call them to repent as normally understood, which involved restitution (in personal offences) and a formal offering of sacrifice in the Temple. He asked only that they accept his message—which offered them the Kingdom. This was the scandal—a fatal scandal for Jesus—of the righteous.[7] Jesus preached forgiveness rather than repentance. And he turned forgiveness into celebration (Luke 15:7, 10, 22-24, 32; 23:43).

The Offence

Traditionally, the message of, the challenge of, Jesus has been modified in every conceivable way. Here is a case in point. Jesus welcomed sinners—without condition. This was shockingly unconventional and a scandal to the righteous. Jesus was too much for the religious authorities of his day. He seems to be too much for religious authority of any day. Always, it seems, sinners can find that gap and encounter the gracious forgiveness and welcome of the Father/Mother—always to the discomfiture of the righteous.

> Why does he eat with tax collectors and sinners? . . . Those who are well have no need of a physician, but those who are sick; I came not to call the righteous, but sinners (Mark 2:16-17).

It was notorious that Jesus was a friend of tax collectors and sinners. This text reflects a conflict between the Jesus movement and other Jews on the issue. Similarly, we may take it that those addressed in Matthew 21:31 ("Truly, I say to you, the tax collectors and the harlots go into the kingdom of God before you") are Jews who deny to tax collectors and sinners the right to hope in God's forgiveness. The offence of the statement is its clear implication that the wretched prostitutes and detested tax collectors, scorned by the educated and refined, are preferred by God to their despisers. True, they are "sick," not only in the eyes of their contemporaries but in the eyes of God, as well. Pharisees would be prepared to accept that God is merciful to sinners; they would not accept the unconditional forgiveness of God implicit in the role of Jesus. In the earliest Jesus movement, the Pharisees are not yet representatives of a Judaism hostile to Christianity. They are Jews who perceived that the Jesus movement was making an enormous and, to them, an unacceptable claim. It was claiming that God takes the part of the poor and the outcast—simply because they are poor, deprived and despised. The rule of God was being inaugurated among the lowly and despised—not among the "righteous." This they could not, and would not, accept.[8]

Theology of the Cross

Mark stands side by side with Paul as a stalwart proclaimer of a *theologia crucis*—a theology of the Cross. And, congenial to modern Christology, the Marcan Jesus is the most human of any. Jesus is Son of God, that is, God-appointed leader of the new covenant people; he is "son of man"—*this man*—the human one who came to serve, the one faithful unto death. One who has come to terms with the Cross (the meaning of his death) can know him and can confess him—like the centurion (15:39). His disciples did not understand him before Calvary. The Christian reader of the first century and of today is being challenged to come to terms with the love of God manifest in the Cross of Jesus.

For Jesus, as for all of us, life was pilgrimage—at more than one level. What Luke had to say of the twelve-year-old is perceptively true: "And Jesus increased in wisdom and in stature and in favor with God and man" (Luke 2:52). His journey was not only from Nazareth to the Jordan, from Galilee to Jerusalem. It was, above all, a journey of faith. Jesus, who knew the Father as no other did, still had to learn what it was the Father asked of him at the end of all. He found himself face to face with the stark reality of the Cross: ". . . not what I will, but what you will." While fully aware that, in everything he did and said, he revealed the true God, he was to find that his last word was to be the revelation of what Paul would call the "foolishness" of God. The man himself was the revelation; his life and his death the medium of his message.

The Pilgrimage

The pilgrimage of Jesus—*the* representative of our God—from a ministry of uninhibited love of humankind to death on a human-provided cross, is the great and ultimate human pilgrimage. No banners there, no colorful procession—despite an ephemeral welcome (Mark 11:1-10, parr.). Just disillusionment, shared by followers: "Jesus was walking ahead of them; and they were amazed, and those who followed were afraid" (10:32). They had caught the smell of disaster; the whiff was clear enough. Popular enthusiasm had waned: Jesus was no messianic warrior but a pacifist for the cause of God. Yet, he had explicitly challenged the religious establishment by his criticism of Temple worship and of observance of Torah. He was a heretic. He had implicitly challenged Rome. He was a rebel. It did not matter that his challenge was totally peaceful and wholly marked by love. He was walking the most precarious walk of all: the walk of one who holds for love in face of those who acknowledge only power—whether naked or subtly disguised. That awesome, and awful, journey to the Cross is comfort to all who have seen in Jesus of Nazareth the image of the invisible God. It is the consolation of all who have found in him the ultimate assurance that God is on *our* side.

Jesus had "set his face to go to Jerusalem" (Luke 9:51). Mark's Gethsemane-scene (14:32-42) shows that he did not fully understand God's way, shows that he did not want to die. His Gethsemane decision was to trust God despite the darkness of his situation. He entrusted to God his own experience of failure: his endeavor to renew Israel was being brutally thwarted. His people had rejected him as they had, formerly, rejected his Father. His cry of God-forsakenness on the cross—"My God, my God, why have you forsaken me?"—speaks the bitterness of his sense of failure. Contempt surrounded the death of Jesus. Archaeology has shown that Golgotha, a disused quarry, was a rubbish-dump. We have sanitized the Way of the Cross and the Cross itself. The reality was sordid. And here we should remind ourselves that, as Christians, we know about God through the humanity of Jesus. We need to accomodate ourselves to the idea of a Supreme Being who can fully reveal himself in this manner.[9]

Jesus had not set out from Galilee to embrace the Cross. Throughout his ministry he had preached the rule of God—God as salvation for humankind. His last, involuntary, sermon was the most eloquent of all. The close of his earthly pilgrimage was to be his unequivocal proclamation of true divinity and true humanity. For, the Cross is God's revelation of himself. It is there he defines himself over against all human caricatures of him. God, in the Cross, is a radical challenge to our *hubris,* our pride. There he is seen to be the *Deus humanissimus*—the God wholly bent on the salvation of humankind.[10] No wonder that Paul can ask, in awe: "Since God did not withold from us the most precious of all gifts, even the life of his own Son to give life to us all, can we not be certain that he would not possibly refuse us whatever else we may need?" (Rom 8:32).

Notes

1. "Note carefully that there is nothing in the Old Testament or New Testament which would imply that Word or Spirit is a *personal counterpart* of *God* in the modern sense of the word *personal.* ["God" as used in the New Testament: the God Jesus called "Father"]. To put it accurately, *Word* is the real condition of possibility, within God, for the existence of anyone or anything outside him, and *Spirit* is the condition of possibility for his accepting and lov-

ing presence with things and persons outside him. Word and Spirit are the conditions of possibility, within the very life of *God*, for his having a counterpart to whom he could speak and with whom he could be involved in a relation of mutual love. The personalization (in the *modern sense*) of Word and Spirit is not undertaken either by the Old Testament or the New Testament and cannot be justified on the basis of either of these texts. Word and Spirit *are personal* not because they are personal counterparts of the Father within the divine life itself but because they are forms of relatedness which *God*, a person, has with a person or persons in our world." John C. Dwyer, *Son of Man and Son of God*. A New Language for Faith (New York: Paulist, 1983) 121–122.

"The New Testament imagery is in itself powerful and flexible although subsequent usage has sometimes given it an alien rigidity. Jesus as the Word of God spoken in eternity and spoken now into history, is personal in the sense that it is God speaking, not in the sense that a person is envisaged in eternity in addition to God. Moreover, it allows easy passage of the imagination from the creative speaking of God in Genesis to the redemptive, recreative speaking of God in the Christ event, while resonating with memories of the Word of God as spoken by the prophets." Monika K. Hellwig, *Jesus, the Compassion of God*. New Perspectives on the Tradition of Christianity (Wilmington, DE: M. Glazier, 1983) 119–120.

2. "Note carefully that in the New Testament it is not the Logos or *Word* which is the personal counterpart of God and the term of his eternal decision not to remain alone. *Jesus* is the counterpart of God, the one whom he has sought and found. The world and its history, natural and human, came into being, so that God might one day greet Jesus as his Son." J. C. Dwyer, *op. cit.*, 122–123.

3. "But note well: Jesus' personal relationship with God cannot be relegated to a place 'outside' of the world and to a time which preceded the concrete human existence of Jesus. Jesus is the only Son of this Father, precisely in his human existence. Jesus' relationship to the Father is not grounded in some timeless substratum of his being which would underlie his outer human reality. What is eternal, 'pre-existent' (the term is unfortunate) is the Word of God, which is *not*, in the *contemporary sense of the word*, the person of Jesus, but is rather God's eternal commitment to be personally present in history. Because God's word is a distinct form of relatedness within the very life of God, history can be *God's own history*. And one good way to describe Jesus would be to call him the reality of the history of God. Jesus is the proof that God cannot be kept out of history and that history has no meaning apart from the presence of God as a participant within it . . . .

"The mystery of Jesus is that in him God communicates himself in a full and unrestricted way. The divinity of Jesus is not some kind of second substance in him, some type of superior reality which would have to be thought of as 'next to' and necessarily in competition with his human reality. Jesus' divinity consists in the fact that he is the human person (in the *contemporary sense* of *person*) who is the perfect counterpart of God and who is therefore *the manifestation and presence of God himself in the world*" J. C. Dwyer, *op. cit.*, 130–131. The substance of christology: "That this man Jesus is the very word and presence of the Father among us, that he is in an absolutely unique sense *of* God and *from* God and that he is therefore in just as unique a sense the *Son* of God." *Ibid.*, 137.

4. "It is quite understandable, within the context of fourth and fifth century thought, that an attempt to define the mysterious nature of Jesus theoretically was made at Chalcedon (451). All the same, it is very dangerous to make such attempts. To attempt to define Jesus' nature is to limit it, to narrow it down, to bring it to a point that may well be too sharp, with the result that Jesus is either underestimated or overestimated." Edward Schillebeeckx, *God is New Each Moment* (New York: The Seabury Press, 1983) 41.

"The process of Christologizing Jesus of Nazareth may indeed 'freeze' or neutralize his message and praxis but lose sight of him and leave us with only a celestial cult mystery: the great Ikon Christ, shunted so far off in a Godward direction (God himself having been edged out of this world of men) that he, too, Jesus Christ, ceases to have any critical impact on the life of the world. To contend for the divinity of Jesus in a world of which God has long since taken his leave may well be a battle lost before it has begun. It also fails to grasp the deepest intention of God's plan of salvation, namely, God's resolve to encounter us 'in fashion as a man,' so that—indeed—we might eventually be enabled to find him. If we mean to honour God's saving purposes we shall submit to the judgment of the man Jesus; only then will we acquire an outlook upon the living God. This will require us to forbear—even in catechesis. To put it starkly: whereas God is bent on showing himself in human form, we on our side slip past this human aspect as quickly as we can in order to admire a 'divine Ikon' from which every trait of the critical prophet has been smoothed away. Thus we 'neutralize' the critical impact of God himself and run the risk simply of adding a new ideology to those which mankind already possesses in such plenty: that is to say, Christology itself! I fear at times that with the keen edge of our credal utterances about Jesus we dull the critical vision of his prophecy, having as it does real consequences for our society and politics. A one-sided apotheosis of Jesus that restricts him exclusively to the divine side actually has the effect of removing from our history a nuisance-figure who would challenge our self-indulgence, and the dangerous memory of some provocative and vital prophesying—is also a way of silencing Jesus the prophet! As against this Christology the words apply: 'Why do you call me "Lord, Lord," and do not do what I tell you? . . . Depart from me, all you workers of iniquity' (Lk 6:46 and 13:27)." Edward Schillebeeckx, *Jesus*. An Experiment in Christology (New York: Crossroad, 1981) 670–671.

5. *Op. cit.*, 43.

6. "The concept of God in [the great councils of the fourth and fifth centuries] is different from that in the Old and New Testaments. In them we have a Greek concept of God which does not stand in any direct relationship to

our earthly time and space. There, too, a quite different image of humanity is used from that in the Bible. Within this conceptual framework of humanity and God (which needs to be criticized in the light of the Bible) these councils, precisely in order to remain faithful in a Hellenistic milieu to the New Testament Jesus Christ, were obliged to speak as they did. Authentic Christians were speaking here—but at the same time they were thinking Greeks. What they did secured and saved the New Testament confession for us. But this does not mean that we must accept the philosophical and anthropological presuppositions of these Greek councils (or a particular model of the incarnation) as the condition for a living and unabbreviated faith in Jesus confessed as the Christ. These councils, from Nicaea to Chalcedon, show us little of the vulnerable man Jesus who also suffered on the cross. In these councils the individual Jew Jesus of Nazareth faded away to give place to the 'one human nature,' ahistorical. Moreover what these councils meant to say was essentially hardened and often distorted in catechesis, preaching and theology. And in church tradition they often functioned as a source of understanding faith almost independent of the New Testament, standing by themselves: they were even used as a more important source than scripture. The crisis in which many contemporary christologies find themselves today seems to me to lie in the fact that for modern men and women the Chalcedon model no longer speaks in human terms and is usually incomprehensible, while as yet there are no new theological models to make clear today the deepest meaning of Chalcedon. Hence all the searching and experimentation in contemporary christology. We cannot begrudge these seeking Christians time to become clear about Jesus, confessed as the Christ, God's only Son, our Lord." Edward Schillebeeckx, *Jesus in Our Western Culture* (London: SCM, 1987) 45–46.

7. E. P. Sanders, *Jesus and Judaism* (London: SCM, 1985) 174–211. James D. G. Dunn, *Jesus, Paul and the Law* (London: SPCK, 1990) 79–81.

8. "There is something subtle and killing in a particular kind of virtue. The subtle vice of 'perfection' has not yet disappeared from church life. People defend so-called unassailable laws, and in so doing injure already vulnerable fellow men and women. Jesus showed that up. The effect of this zeal is often to deprive men and women of room to breathe. Jesus opposes worldly practice when the law has the effect of excluding the other person. If the law reduces people to despair, it forfeits all authority. For Jesus, the poor and the outcast are the criterion of whether the law is functioning creatively or destructively, as the will of God for the benefit of men and women." Edward Schillebeeckx, *Church*. The Human Story of God (London: SCM, 1990) 117.

9. "On the cross Jesus shared in the brokenness of our world. This means that God determines in absolute freedom, down the ages, who and how he wills to be in his deepest being, namely, a God of men and women, an ally in our suffering and our absurdity, and also an ally in the good that we do. In his own being he is a God for us. I therefore can no longer see any significance to the classic difference between 'God in himself' and 'God for us.'

"In the New Testament there is a theological redefinition of various concepts of God, and also a redefinition of what it is to be human. God accepts men and women unconditionally, and precisely through this unconditional acceptance he transforms them and calls them to repentance and renewal. Therefore the cross is also a judgment on our own views: a judgment on our ways of living out the meaning of being human and being God. Here is revealed ultimately and definitively the humanity of God, the nucleus of Jesus' message of the kingdom of God: God who comes into his own in the world of human beings for their healing and happiness, even through suffering." E. Schillebeeckx, *op. cit.,* 126.

10. "When God becomes man in Jesus of Nazareth, he not only enters into the finitude of man, but in his death on the cross also enters into the situation of man's godforsakenness. In Jesus he does not die the natural death of a finite being, but the violent death of the criminal on the cross, the death of complete abandonment by God. The suffering in the passion of Jesus is abandonment, rejection by God, his Father. God does not become a religion, so that man participates in him by corresponding religious thoughts and feelings. God does not become a law, so that man participates in him through obedience to a law. God does not become an ideal, so that man achieves community with him through constant striving. He humbles himself and takes upon himself the eternal death of the godless and the forsaken, so that all the godless and the forsaken can experience communion with him . . .

"If God has taken upon himself death on the cross, he has also taken upon himself all of life and real life, as it stands under death, law and guilt. In so doing he makes it possible to accept life whole and entire and death whole and entire. Man is taken up, without limitations and conditions, into the life and suffering, the death and resurrection of God, and in faith participates corporeally in the fullness of God." Jürgen Moltmann, *The Crucified God.* The Cross of Christ as the Foundation and Criticism of Christian Theology (London: SCM, 1974) 276–277.

4
THE FOOLISH GOD
THE GOD OF PAUL

For the word of the cross is folly (1 Cor 1:18).

Paul was keenly conscious of a formidable difficulty at the heart of the Christian message. After all, Jesus had been condemned by the sanhedrin, the supreme religious authority of Judaism, and one of the charges against him was that he was a messianic pretender. If the reaction of Peter at Caesarea Philippi to the very suggestion that the Messiah might suffer and die was indignant rejection (Mark 8:31-33) how much more unacceptable for any Jew to acknowledge as Messiah one whom God had abandoned to a shameful death. As for the non-Jew: it was asking too much to recognize a savior in that helpless victim on a cross. When Paul declared: "We preach Christ crucified, a stumbling-block to Jews and folly to Gentiles" (1 Cor 1:23), he spoke from wry experience. He will not compromise. He wants to know nothing "except Jesus Christ and him crucified" (2:2) because it was just here he had come to discern the power and the wisdom of God (cf. 1:24). Nor does Paul view the resurrection of Jesus as a "saving operation"; he would regard the resurrection as inherent in the Cross. The resurrection showed up the Cross in its true light and demonstrated that "the foolishness of God is wiser than men, and the weakness of God is stronger than men" (1:25). Paul would not draw a veil over the scandal of the Cross.

No one can properly evaluate Paul's theological achievement without a sympathetic appreciation of the challenge he faced. It fell to him to transform a Jewish charge levelled at the implication of the shameful death of Jesus, "Cursed be every one who hangs on a tree" (Deut 21:23) into a statement of God's saving purpose: "Christ redeemed us from the curse of the law, having become a curse for us" (Gal 3:13). Paul is being consciously paradoxical. He uses the word "curse" because it was the basis of the opposing charge. In no way does he suggest that Jesus—even as our surrogate—became, in some sense, object of God's "anger." By becoming "a curse for us" Jesus manifests at once his own love and the love of his Father, and ours.

Theology of the Cross

"Theology of the Cross" sounds grim. Yet, theology of the Cross, as proclaimed by Paul, is positive and full of hope. That is because the starting-point is the graciousness of God—or, as he termed it, the "foolishness" of God. The foolishness of God, expressed in the Cross of Jesus, shows God's commitment to humankind. He is indeed a God bent on the salvation of humankind.

In face of folly-and-scandal obstacle, Paul would proclaim the Cross—because the Cross showed forth, with stark clarity, the saving will and the saving power of God. One may ask: Why should the death of Jesus have power to save? How does that saving come about? Paul saw that the answer must lie with God. "God was in Christ, reconciling the world to himself" (2 Cor 5:19)—there is the answer. God is active in the Cross. Reconciliation is *God's* deed, not ours. God "through Christ reconciled us to himself" (5:18). Salvation is reconciliation with God because salvation means that the human person is, at last, fully, wholly human. This can be only when one is in complete communion with God. Attainment of true humanness is, in the last resort, God's achievement. For, the answer to the primal human temptation to be like God is to let God be God in one's life. That is the lesson of the Cross.

MAN and GOD

On the cross God shows what it is to be human. God's Son dramatically demonstrates the radical powerlessness of the human being. He shows that we are truly human when we accept our humanness, when we face up to the fact that we are not masters of our fate. As Jesus was stripped of his clothes so, too, he displayed a humanness stripped of every illusion. And nowhere more than there did he manifest himself as the one come to serve. On the cross Jesus manifested himself as the one who had yielded himself wholly to his God. The Cross offers the authentic definition of humanness: God's definition. There he, starkly, firmly, reminds us of who and what we are. On the cross God defines the human being as creature—not to crush or humiliate but that he may be, as Creator, wholly with his creature. On its own, humankind has indeed reason to fear. With God, in total dependence on God, there is no room for fear. The resurrection of Jesus makes that clear. For the resurrection is God's endorsement of the definition of MAN made on the cross. And it is God's endorsement of the definition of God made there.

In the Cross God calls in question every one of our vaunted human pretensions. The God revealed in Jesus makes no claims for himself, he bears no titles. He is the God prepared to be least of all, the God who serves. He is the God who has entered, wholly, into rejection and humiliation and suffering. He is the God present in human life where to human eyes he is absent. He is the God who is not aloof from death. We, Christians, meet our God in the *man* Jesus of Nazareth. We must admit to meeting our *God* on a cross. We must be prepared to let God be God. Our God is a *Deus humanissimus,* a thoroughly human God, and he will not be God on any other terms.[1]

The Claim of God

In chapters 1–3 of Romans, Paul paints a gloomy picture indeed: a human world estranged from God. The tyrant *Sin* had got a firm grip on *sarx* ("flesh"), the human condition of weakness. Paradoxically, this weakness is the fatal human illusion of independence, of being able to go it alone. That was the primal sin: to be like God (Gen 3:1-7). That striving for autonomy was disastrous because humankind cannot make it without God. Paul is sure that salvation is, must be, God's deed: it cannot be earned. And he is sure that salvation can be ours only by means of a faith that is openness to God's gift.[2]

God's *dikaiosynē*, his "righteousness" is, indeed, his laying claim to us; it is an assertion of his rights.[3] This assertion, however, is made not in a spirit of domination but wholly on our behalf. We had been slaves of the tyrants *Hamartia* (Sin) and *Thanatos* (Death). Now God declares: "You are mine!" Where another lord might declare: "I am your lord—obey!" our God says to us: "I am your Father/Mother, you are my dear children—come to me!." For our part we must let it be; we must say our "yes" to God's claim on us. That is *faith*: saying yes to God, letting God be God *for us*. It is through Jesus Christ that God makes his claim. He is our God "who did not spare his own Son but gave him up for us all" (Rom 8:32). That, more than anything else, shows the character of God's lordship.

The "Wrath" of God

Does not Paul himself temper somewhat the graciousness of God? He speaks once (Rom 1:18) of the "wrath of God," divine retribution, while "wrath," retribution, is found several times in his writings. One needs carefully to discern what is at issue here. God's "wrath" has, too often, been invoked in ways that do little credit to God and immense hurt to men and women. In secular Greek *orgē* is a natural impulse or mood, usually anger. Biblical Greek introduces a fresh angle, involving the reaction of the divinity to our sin. In biblical Greek God's emotive reaction to human disobedience and stupitidy is vaguely expressed anthropomorphically by this word which translated the Hebrew *aph* (burning anger) and *hema* (wrath). In the New Testament *orgē* refers often enough to God's "wrath." Noteworthy, however, is the fact that the verb *orgizomai* (to be angry) is never used in the Bible with God as subject. *Orgē* is to be thought of as an impersonal quality: effect (*effectus*) rather than emotion (*affectus*). The evolution in the perception of divine anger, from our earliest evidence to Paul, has been excellently traced by C. H. Dodd:

> In the oldest parts of the Old Testament the anger of Yahweh displays itself in thunder, earthquake, pestilence and the like. The

prophets took up this idea, but rationalized it by teaching that disaster is not an outbreak of irresponsible anger, but an expression of the outraged justice of God. There is no disaster but deserved disaster. Thus "the Wrath of God" is taken out of the sphere of the purely mysterious, and brought into the sphere of cause and effect: sin is the cause, disaster the effect. At the same time they taught that Yahweh was loving and merciful, and desirous of saving his people from disaster, by saving them from sin which is the cause of the disaster. . . . While there is a tension, not wholly resolved, between the wrath and the mercy of God, it would be fair to say that in speaking of wrath and judgment the prophets and psalmists have their minds mainly on events, actual or expected, conceived as the inevitable result of sin; and when they speak of mercy they are thinking mainly of the personal relation between God and his people. Wrath is the effect of human sin: mercy is not the effect of human goodness, but is inherent in the character of God. When they speak of his righteousness . . . they find it consummated in a merciful deliverance of his people from the power and oppression of sin—in fact from "the Wrath."

Thus the way is open for a further development in which anger as an attitude of God to men disappears, and his love and mercy become all-embracing. This is, I believe, the purport of the teaching of Jesus, with its emphasis on limitless forgiveness and on God's fatherly kindness to "the unthankful and evil." In substance, Paul agrees with this, teaching that God loves us while we were yet sinners (Rom 5:8) and that it is his kindness that leads us to repentance (2:4). But he retains the concept of "the Wrath of God" (Rom 1:18; cf Eph 5:6) (which does not appear in the teaching of Jesus) . . . not to describe the attitude of God to man, but to describe an inevitable process of cause and effect in a moral universe.[4]

Salvation

When it comes to salvation, Paul knows no distinction (Rom 3:22): faith in Jesus Christ is now and henceforth the only path to salvation for Jew and Gentile alike. All humankind had "fallen short of the glory of God" (3:23), that is to say, were no longer truly in the image of God. The root of our failure is the human propensity to put non-gods in the place of God. When we acknowledge God's claim on us the image is restored. Because he lays claim to us as sinners we are justified "as a gift" (3:24). By letting God be "just," by letting him be gracious in our regard, we are renewed, we are re-created. God's saving power—that is what "grace" means—brings about the new creation. By relying solely on Christ, God's saving presence among us, we are set free from our attempts to make ourselves acceptable by creating congenial gods. For Paul, it is Christ who reveals the power of God, particularly in his death. In him the *dikaiosynē,* the saving lordship of God, has put in an appearance and is really here.[5]

The Faithful Friend

> While we were yet sinners, at the right time, Christ died for the ungodly. . . God shows his love for us in that while we were yet sinners Christ died for us (Rom 5:6, 8).

It is the clearest possible proof that God loves humankind, sinful as we are. "The ungodly": Jesus died for those who were estranged from God. Paul stresses the love revealed in the fact that God, in Jesus, went to such lengths on our behalf.

> If while we were yet sinners we were reconciled to God by the death of his Son, much more, now that we are reconciled, shall we be saved by his life. Not only so, but we also rejoice in God through our Lord Jesus Christ, through whom we have now received our reconciliation (5:10-11).

We have received our reconciliation because on the cross the human person is truly human, nothing other than God's creature. By saying yes to God's deed in Jesus—faith—we acknowledge that reality. Reconciliation: God wants us to be his *friends.* To be set right with God means to have him as a faithful friend.

Children of God

> All who are led by the Spirit of God are children of God . . . When we cry "Abba! Father!" it is the Spirit himself bearing witness with our spirit that we are children of God, and if children then heirs, heirs of God and fellow heirs with Christ, provided we suffer with him in order that we may also be glorified with him (8:14-17).

The Spirit—God's loving presence in our world—has brought about a second transformation, the transformation of "slave" into "child." God's Spirit makes us members of God's family. It lets us address God as Jesus did: Abba. If we share God as Father with Jesus, then we are children of God and members of God's family. That is our human destiny—but we had lost sight of it. The Spirit must bring the Christian to an awareness of this remarkable situation. The God who has adopted us as his children awakens in us an awareness of that fact and then gently helps us in our wondering acknowledgment of that fact: Abba! "Provided we suffer with him": suffering at the hands of a world dominated by "flesh" is a sign that we no longer belong to that world. Suffering—"if we share in his Cross": Paul will not hear of a "Christianity" which claims to have found union with the risen Christ and yet seeks to avoid the Cross in life *now*.

Baptism

In Romans 6:1-11 Paul turns to union with Christ through baptism; he does so in a search for the basis of Christian morality. He had set aside the law as being, at best, a signpost to conduct, offering no practical help. He had stressed that justification was by faith apart from works of law. Indeed, he had just declared that where sin abounded, grace abounds much more (5:20). Is there any good reason, then, why a Christian should be good? Paul's way of meeting the difficulty is to start from a consideration of baptism as sacrament of initiation into the Christian life.

He asks, "How can we who have died to sin still live in it?" (v. 2) His point is that, because a Christian is one removed from the domain where sin rules—set free from the tyrant Sin—then, as far as sin is concerned, we are dead. Christians recognize the lordship of Christ, a lordship that demands our total dedication to him.

> Do you not know that all of us who have been baptized into Christ Jesus were baptized into his death? We were buried therefore with him by baptism into death, so that as Christ was raised from the dead by the glory of the Father, we too might walk in newness of life (6:3-4).

For Paul, Christian baptism, initiation rite into the Christian community, is also much more. Baptism is a concrete expression of faith; if faith is acceptance of the crucified Lord so, in effect, is baptism. "Buried with him": readily enough suggested by the rite of immersion baptism—a rich symbolism. The one to be baptised goes down into the water, as Jesus descended into the grave of death; and then rises out of the watery grave, as Jesus was raised from death. The Christian's emergence to new life is at the cost of dying to sin, as Jesus died to sin. It is achieved by the power of God, as Jesus was raised by the Father's power. Our hope—an assured hope—is that one day we *might* walk in newness of life; that one day we may share fully in the new life which he won for us. Again (v. 5) Paul insists that we *shall* be united with Christ in his glorified life. He never forgets—or lets us forget—that, in this age, Christian life is life under the Cross. Jesus is our Lord here and now—in this vale of tears.

> We know that our old self was crucified with him so that the sinful body might be destroyed, and we might no longer be enslaved to sin. For he who died is free from sin (6:6-7).

We are "crucified" with Jesus when we acknowledge the Crucified One as Lord. By that faith I "die" to any self-assertiveness or "boasting" in terms of my own achievements and merits. The "body" is the whole self; it is a "sinful body" because distorted by the baleful power of sin. For one "in Christ," however, that distortion no longer operates. That is why "he who has died" has been set free from the power of sin. For the Christian this "death" leads to life: "We shall also live with him" (v. 8). Note: *shall* live— Paul's theology of the Cross will not yield to a seductive "theology of glory."

> The death he died he died to sin, once for all, but the life he lives he lives to God. So you also must consider yourselves dead to sin and alive to God in Christ Jesus (6:10-11).

What is meant by the statement "Christ died to sin?" It means, simply, that Jesus died rather than sin. That is why in 8:3 we read that God "by sending his own Son in the likeness of sinful flesh . . . condemned sin in the flesh." The claim of Sin against Jesus failed utterly, and Sin was routed. The Christian, dying to sin as Christ did, can share in that once-for-all, decisive occasion and participate in the victory: dead to sin, alive to God *in Christ Jesus.*

Destiny

> Those whom he foreknew he also predestined to be conformed to the image of his Son, in order that he might be the first-born among many brethren (8:29).

Words of Scripture have been, and are, misunderstood again and again. In one respect that should not surprise because the word is not always simple and obvious; Paul, in particular, can be hard to fathom. What is upsetting is that misinterpretation, too often, leads to an ungracious image of God, as here in respect to "predestination." Paul does declare that God "foreknew," meaning God's eternal choice to be for us; and God "predestined," destined us to belong to the Christian community. "The terms do not refer to some limitation on our freedom, nor do they refer to some arbitrary decision by God that some creatures are to be denied all chance of salvation. They simply point to the fact that God knows the end to which he will bring his creation, namely redemption, and that that destiny is firmly set in his purposes. God has already set the destiny of creation: that destiny is redemption (v. 21)—In that sense Paul can speak of 'pre-*destination*.' It means, just as the word says, that the *destiny* has already been set, and that destiny is the final redemptive transformation of reality. Therefore, the good news is that our destiny lies no longer in our own hands but in the hands of an all-powerful and loving God, whose purpose is redemption."[6] That, so obviously, is Paul's meaning. The context of the statement makes it all the more hard to understand how such perverse and damaging theories of predestination could ever have been devised. One has to question, seriously, the image of God entertained by those who devised them. He was a God far removed from the foolish God of Paul.

God for Us

And the context is the peroration of 8:31-39. That remarkable declaration of his certainty of salvation is a matchless statement of

Paul's Gospel. It tells us that God's love is *like this*. It assures us that here is the God who has laid claim to us and has given us a claim on him.

> What can we possibly add to what we have already said? God is caring for us, who or what can *possibly* harm us?
>
> Since God did not withhold from us the most precious of all gifts, even the life of his own Son to give life to us all, can we not be certain that he would not *possibly* refuse us whatever else we may need?
>
> When God has chosen us to be his special friends, can anyone's misunderstanding or even rejection *possibly* have any hold on us? Who can bring any real charge against us? Certainly *not* the God who pardons us from all charges! Who can ever really condemn us? Certainly *not* the merciful Christ Jesus!
>
> Why, not only did he actually die for us. He also rose from death to abide in the presence of God himself, where he prays unceasingly on our behalf.
>
> Thus, nothing whatsoever can take us away from the love of Jesus. Even if we are anxious, distressed, or attacked, even if we are without food and clothing, even if we are being threatened or even assaulted, still nothing can ever take us away from him.
>
> After all, the psalm says: "For your sake, O Lord, we die each day and are counted as sheep for the slaughter." And such trials as these are sent to us only so that, in the end, we may overcome them—overcome them through the strength of his love.
>
> So, I repeat that I am *absolutely sure* of this: No experience whatsoever in dying or living, nothing in the realm of ideas or spirits, nothing in the realm of earthbound reality, nothing in the future, nor any kind of power, nothing concerning the stars of heaven or creatures of earth, can ever—ever—possibly take us away from God's love shining forth upon us in Jesus.[7]

We learn at once who God is: he is *God for us*. It is as good a definition of God as we might hope for. He is the loving God who created us and called us to be his daughters and his sons. The question: "Will he not also give us all things with him?" can have one answer only. The giving of his Son shows, beyond doubt, that God is in deadly earnest. Father and Son are prepared to go to any length to save MAN from himself. God gave his Son without precondition; he took the risk. The death of his Son was, at the deepest level, a sacrifice made by God.

Here Mark 12:1-12 is illuminating. The parable of the Wicked Vinedressers is specifically designed to bring out the theological significance of the death of Jesus. It is allegory. The vineyard is Israel; the tenants become, at the end, the chief priests and scribes and elders. The rejected and maltreated servants are the prophets. The climax is the sending of the son. It is the master's last card: "They will respect my son." The last thing the master desired was the death of his son. The message is unmistakable. God did not desire the death of his Son; he did not need the death of his Son. He took a colossal risk: "God did not spare his own Son."

In Romans 8:33-34 we have two questions with ironical answers. Who can bring a charge? God—who justifies! It is really another way of putting the question: "If God is for us, who is against us?" Can we imagine that the God who, in our helplessness, has, at such a cost, taken his saving initiative, is now going to be our Judge? And who will condemn us? Christ Jesus, who died for us, who intercedes for us! Again it is another way of putting a question, this time the question, "Who will separate us from the love of Christ?" Christ's love for us is dramatically manifest in his sacrificial death and in his efficacious intercession. Tribulation and distress cannot separate us from the love of Christ. No trials of our human lot can come between the Christian and that unyielding love.

The Christian? God is *for us*—God of humankind. God created MAN to be his counterpart in creation. He waited for an unequivocal yes. That yes was spoken by and in Jesus of Nazareth. Now God could, God would, "restore all things in Christ." The Father of our Lord Jesus Christ is Savior of humankind. God has walked among us in Jesus of Nazareth. *Ho logos sarx egeneto.*

Notes

1. See John C. Dwyer, *Son of God and Son of Man* (New York: Paulist, 1983) 164–173.

2. "A corollary of thinking about God the Creator, who, as Lord, is free to dispose over his creation as he sees fit and who, as human history has shown,

has disposed over it not as it deserved but in gracious overlooking of his creatures' rebellion, is the unavoidable fact that human beings, as creatures, are never the rulers of their own destinies. Only the Creator, not the creature, is fit to exercise lordship. That means that as Paul understands human creatures everyone is subject to some lordship, to some power which one is forced to serve. A creature is not free to be its own lord, to dispose over its own life. . . . Paul is clear that since Adam the power to which creatures are subjected is sin. Because the creature is enslaved to that power, the creature is powerless to effect his or her own deliverance from it. Only a force stronger than sin can deliver the creature from sin." Paul Achtemeier, *Romans* (Atlanta: John Knox Press, 1985) 16.

3. The current translations—"righteousness" or "justice"—of the word *dikaiosynē* are not adequate; worse than that, they are misleading. The "righteousness of God" is regularly taken to be a divine attribute. Paul thinks of an act or activity of God. And when he says that "the righteousness of God is revealed" he means that God's activity is manifest in the field of human experience. This becomes clear when we look at the background which for Paul is, of course, the Old Testament. Behind the word *dikaiosynē* in the Septuagint (the pre-Christian Greek translation of the Hebrew Scriptures) is the Hebrew *sedaqa*. The root verb *sadaq* means "to put in the right" and also "to vindicate" a person who has been victimized. A judge is not a just judge by upholding an abstract legal standard, but because he vindicates the cause of the oppressed—he is champion of "the widow and orphan." His "righteousness" is seen in the "justification" of those who are victims of oppression. It is true that the term *dikaiosynē* carries, too, the connotation of an assertion of rights. What we should bear in mind is that it, or any term, when predicated of God, always means something quite different from its meaning in a merely human context.

4. *The Epistle of St Paul to the Romans* (London: Collins, 1959) 49–50. Jürgen Moltmann observes: "What the Old Testament terms *the wrath of God* does not belong in the category of the anthropomorphic transference of lower human emotions to God, but in the category of the divine *pathos*. His wrath is injured love and therefore a mode of his reaction to men. Love is the source and the basis of the possibility of the wrath of God . . . As injured love, the wrath of God is not something that is inflicted, but a divine suffering of evil. It is a sorrow which goes through his opened heart. He suffers in his passion for his people." *The Crucified God* (London: SCM, 1974) 272.

There is a real sense in which one can rightly speak of God's *anger*—when anger is a reaction, motivated by strong love for people, to a situation of intolerable injustice. Thus, Albert Nolan can write: "God is angry, God is absolutely furious, about what is being done to people in South Africa today. I say that without any hesitation. There is simply no other way of communicating or expressing the barbarous excess of suffering, the magnitude of the evil and the seriousness of our human responsibility for what is happening in our country. . . . God is present in our situation in a mood of anger and indignation. This is no mere religious speculation. The anger of God has become visible for all to see in the anger of the people." *God in South Africa*. The Challenge of the Gospel (Grand Rapids/London: Eerdmans/CIIR, 1988) 105.

5. "We know God not by reflecting on his immutable essence but by hearkening to his voice, by seeing his historical action and by becoming part of his creative engagement with the world and with human beings. For Paul, no less than God himself is at stake in Jesus. In Jesus, God becomes truly, finally, definitively God, because in him God has reconciled the world to himself." J. C. Dwyer, *op. cit.*, 128.

6. P. Achtemeier, *Romans*, 144.

It may help to view "predestination" as the firm *promise* of God: "The basis or grounds for hope that is offered to us in the Bible are the *promises* of an all-powerful God. The Bible is not a book about a salvation that has been achieved and finalized in the past; the Bible is about the promise of salvation in the future. There are stories about powerful saving events, about victories over the powers of evil, but they are not final, at least for us they are not final. We still stand in need of salvation, and the victories of the past are for us signs, symbols or promises of a salvation that is yet to come. Even Jesus' victory on the cross was not final as a victory. It was the definitive revelation, the definitive promise of a final victory over the powers of evil. The Bible is the story of that promise. The Word of God is fundamentally always a word of promise." A. Nolan, *op. cit.*, 116–117.

7. Paraphrase by Edith Pennoyer Livermore.

EPILOGUE

What is a frail mortal, that you should be mindful of him, a human being, that you should take notice of him? . . . Yet you have made him little less than a god (Ps 8:4-5 [REV]).

THE GRIEVING GOD

The psalmist gazed on the broad sweep of the sky and across the earth to the distant horizon. He looked at puny MAN and wondered—"you have made *him* little less than a god!" *We* realize that earth is but one planet in our galaxy, that it is an infinitesimally tiny speck in a vast universe. And we wonder that the Creator of the universe chooses not to be alone. There may be other creatures in other worlds with whom he has dialogue. We do not know. But we do know that he has called humankind into being, freely and of set purpose. Freely, because freedom is an essential attribute of God; freedom is a supreme value of our God. He has made us free and he meticulously respects our freedom. Often one hears the complaint: if God be God, why is our world in such a mess? Why does he not move to clean up the mess? The answer is, precisely, God's respect for human freedom. He might wave his magic wand. The cost is too high, and he will not exact the price. The cost of that radical transformation is sacrifice of freedom. God might have programmed our world. But he does not choose to converse with robots. "Is the arm of the Lord shortened?" The course of history might suggest that he has lost control of his creation. The truth is, the verdict on creation—"God saw all that he had made and, behold, it was very good"—is a verdict that only God can pass.

We can glimpse but "the outskirts of his ways." He has had the first word; he will have the last.

In the meantime God is ever the caring God. He grieves over abuse of freedom, over the dire result of human sin. Sin does not affect God in himself; sin hurts God only in his creatures. He grieves over the havoc it wreaks on his beloved children. It is understandable that humans who, perforce, think of God in human terms, should have imagined the "wrath" of God. A hurt God reacting in terms of the flood might be intelligible to humans. Yet, even then, he did not make good on his threat utterly to destroy humankind. Eventually, it would be understood that God is never a destroyer. "For all existing things are dear to you and you hate nothing that you have created—why else would you have made it?" (Wis 11:24 [REV]). Nevertheless, the notion of an angry God persisted. Even today there are those who would maintain that AIDS is God's plague on sexual permissiveness. There seems to be a pervese human streak which is intent on cutting God down to size; there is an urgency to brand him with some of the less attractive traits of our humanness. God has so much to put up with!

What one finds encouraging in the Genesis stories is the inconsistency of God. The God who had determined to launch the flood takes such great care to preserve "the seed of all living things." He is the God who makes a solemn promise to Noah and invented a reminder of his promise: the bow in the clouds. Clothing the man and woman, a protective mark on a murderer, the careful closing of the hatch on Noah and his crew. The clues are there. He is *this* kind of God, and none other. There is his grieving. Above all there is his yearning. Let us make MAN. He will not be alone. He wills to share. He is God *for us*. Our God deserves better than the insult of ungracious caricature. He deserves the compliment of carefree trust in his graciousness. "He knows what is in MAN." And he is prepared to put up with us—to the end.

THE SUFFERING GOD

There ever has been the human temptation to shape God in our image, to seek to manipulate God. Though the primal command "Have dominion" gave no mandate for human dominion over humans, that form of dominion readily became a reality of human culture. And, readily, authority structures, civil and religious, invoked the sanction of God. The "divine right of kings" was not only a feature of Christendom; it has, in one fashion or other, featured in many human cultures. It was assumed that God had issued, to the establishment, a blank check. God became champion of the privileged, supporter of the status quo. After all, God is the prime aristocrat and upholder of aristocracy!

Happily, some in Israel mounted a challenge. God is not the God of the establishment; he cannot be God of unjust systems. God had longed for, waited for the challenge. He waited, because he would not force. Wearied by passive subservience, pained by a religion that invoked him in support of oppression, he welcomed those who challenged the false God foisted on them. He rejoiced that there were children of his who understood, who recognized the kind of God he is. He stepped by the "great" and welcomed those who cried out to him in their crying out against the caricature of him.

He responded by giving voice to his pain at his people's rejection of him, his sorrow that the people, by and large, had gone astray. Israel was his people: I am your God, you are my people. He had established a covenant with his people—"my covenant, which you broke." They had spurned him, had gone their own way. Their stubbornness could not wear him down. Paul had understood when, against all logic, he maintained: "all Israel will be saved." Why? "Because the gifts and call of God are irrevocable" (Rom 11:26, 29). There is the comfort for humans. All are called to be children of God. He is faithful, though all prove unfaithful. He is ever Parent, though we be fickle children.

God is God of compassion—he suffers *with* his suffering children. Human pain, human woe, are not of his devising. Pain is of the web and woof of human life—not a punishment imposed on humankind. "Behold, it is very good." God alone can see the whole of creation—"good," that is, purposeful. Pain and death are part of that world—not only of the human world. Why? There is mystery. To view pain and death as punishment inflicted by a "just" God is to demean God. That has been the way of religious tradition—not the way of the genial authors of Genesis. We honor

God by accepting our human lot as challenge, challenge to look above and raise our eyes beyond pain and mortality. We are helped, immeasurably, if we look to a God of compassion who is with us in our woe and in our death. He is the God who waits to wipe away all tears. Like little children we come, tear-stained, to our God that she may comfort. A little child may not know why she or he may hurt—but knows that there is solace, and the hurt is forgotten. But the pain is real.

Strangest of all, most comforting of all, God bears the burden of human sin. That is God's decision after the flood. He is wearied by human sin; he bears with it. Birth, new life, comes out of pain. God is pregnant with life, Mother of new creation. There is one answer only to the evil that is sin—and to all evil. Violence can never be the answer. Nothing but love, the infinitely patient divine love, can absorb evil and put it out of commission. God does not suffer in silence. He protests against any manipulation of him. But he suffers—in the manner in which *God* may suffer. He feels and shares the pain inflicted in his name on the weak and vulnerable. So many have been broken, so many lives have been shattered in the name of God. Throughout history, to our day, God has been dishonored. He has been *wearied* beyond measure. Because, too often and with frightening consistency, religious observance has been denial of or suppression of human values. Any depreciation of human values is denial of the God of humankind.

THE CRUCIFIED GOD

"God was in Christ, reconciling the world to himself." As Christians we see our God in Jesus of Nazareth. If we are to let God be God, we must let Jesus be Jesus. Christology—theological understanding of Jesus Christ—cannot be unveiling of *mystery*. We must let the mystery abide. And the mystery *is* the person Jesus of Nazareth. To diminish his human reality is to veil the mystery, to screen from sight the God who should shine through him. Christology has tended to do just that. We need to acknowledge a vulnerable Jesus if we are to meet our vulnerable God. The mystery of Jesus is that in him God communicates himself in a full and unrestricted way. The divinity of Jesus means that he is the human person who is the perfect counterpart of God and, therefore, that he is the manifestation and presence of God himself in the world.

Jesus of Nazareth, one time disciple of John the Baptist, soon became his own man. His distinctive approach was motivated, dictated in fact, by his unique understanding of his Abba—Father. His lifestyle showed him to be, what he really was, revelation of the Father. As such he had come to serve. He who had facile authority (*exousia*) over evil forces and over nature had no authority over people, because he chose not to have. He was reflecting God's delicate respect for human freedom. He showed the presence of God most keenly in his attitude to sinners. They were sick people, he was the physician. He would call them from sin and into life. He invited them into his company; he had tablefellowship, communion, with them. Why? Because *his* God "rejoices more over one sinner who repents than over ninety-nine righteous people!" No wonder he was scandal to the righteous. They could not acknowledge him because they could not recognize his Abba. The God of Jesus is God of the lowly, the despised.

Seen like that, the ultimate revelation of God in the death of Jesus has a logic to it, a certain inevitability. In Jesus God had surrendered himself to humankind—the climax of his wrestling with his people. The grieving God, the suffering God, had become the crucified God. Mark is perceptive when he has his centurion look upon the corpse of a tortured victim and declare: "Indeed this man was the Son of God" (15:39).

The career of Jesus did not end on the cross. The resurrection is God's endorsement of the definitions of both God and humankind which became real on the cross. For, just as the death of Jesus cannot be detached from his life, so, too, his resurrection cannot be detached from his career and death. Because he was raised from the dead, Jesus holds decisive significance for us. Because of the fact of his resurrection we know that meaningless death—and, often, meaningless life—has meaning. Jesus died with the cry on his lips, "My God, my God, why have you abandoned me?" The sequel was to show that God had never forsaken Jesus. We have the assurance that he will never abandon us. While, unlike his immediate disciples, we do not follow the steps of Jesus from Galilee to Jerusalem, we do join his human pilgrimage from birth to death.

His word of promise is that we shall follow him beyond death to share his rest (cf. Heb 12:2). We shall know our Abba at last and become wholly his children—that is our pre-destination.

THE FOOLISH GOD

A crucified God is a foolish God—Paul has said as much. Paul could do so because he perceived that the foolishness of God is the only wisdom. That wisdom was demonstrated on the cross. Where is God? The God absent to human eyes was most present at Calvary. A God of paradox, surprising us. A God displaying *his* power. The wisdom is the saving will and the saving power of God. The saving power is reconciliation. The Cross shows a helpless Jesus wholly turned to God—humanness wholly open to God. The Cross shows Jesus as, radically, Son of God—and MAN as child of God. The Cross shows the earnestness of a gracious God, shows that there is no limit to his desire to win humankind to himself. In the Cross he has put in his claim—his call for our surrender to his parental love.

Humankind stands in need of redemption. Paul was very clear on that score. God took the initiative. He laid claim to us and has given us a claim on him. He is *God for us*—the loving God who created us and called us to be his daughters and his sons. The giving of the Son shows, beyond doubt, that God is in deadly earnest. God is ever Father of the "prodigal son"—who looks eagerly for the homecoming of the child, who is ready to take off and embrace him fondly when he appears on the horizon. Thanks to the foolishness of God, reconciliation is not our task or our achievement. It is gift of a loving Parent.

"Reconciliation" is the key-word. Throughout the Bible rings the anguished cry of a humankind gone astray. And it is only too humanly understandable that there should be a frantic scramble to effect reconciliation with God—through cult and ritual, through scrupulous observance of law. Always there was the more enlightened recognition that reconciliation was God's deed (e.g., Lam 5:21). Paul is following a thoroughly Jewish tradition when he insists on this without remainder. He had come to understand that God had ever longed to reconcile humankind to himself.

"God rejoices more over one sinner who repents. . . ." Jesus makes no apology. He proclaims an outrageous God who is more concerned with the helpless than with self-satisfied righteous. This was a God with whom Saul had to come to terms. And Paul found him in the Cross of Jesus.